Teaching Tool

for

Hallahan and Kauffman

Exceptional Learners
Introduction to Special Education

Eighth Edition

Interactive Companion

prepared by

Kristin A. Lundgren
Peabody College
Vanderbilt University

Allyn and Bacon
Boston   London   Toronto   Sydney   Tokyo   Singapore

ISBN 0-205-33799-6

Printed in the United States of America

10 9 8 7 6 5 4 3 2 1   04 03 02 01 00

Table of Contents

Appendix
Sample Syllabus Incorporating Media Assets

SPED 1010   Introduction to Exceptionality   Fall 2000

INTRODUCTION

The Interactive Companion for Daniel P. Hallahan and James M. Kauffman's *Exceptional Learners: Introduction to Special Education, Eighth Edition* can provide exciting opportunities to explore Special Education through video and audio clips and the endless Web sites related to education and teaching. Multimedia can be an instructive and supplementary tool not only for teaching but for learning as well. Audio and video clips demonstrate, and illustrate, the concepts discussed in the text. In addition, the Interactive Companion features quality Web sites and has placed them within the context of the Hallahan and Kauffman textbook, and more importantly, ties them to the learning objectives of each chapter.

The purpose of this Teaching Tool is to help you integrate the Interactive Companion into your own teaching style and classroom environment. The Teaching Tool is also designed to help you connect the media assets on the CD-ROM with the content your students are learning through your lectures and their textbook. The goal of this supplement is to allow you to use the Interactive Companion to its full benefit, for your teaching and your students' learning.

What is the Interactive Companion?

The Allyn & Bacon Interactive Companion is an exciting new way to learn that expands the traditional text by using the latest in multimedia. When your students buy an Allyn & Bacon Interactive Companion, they receive a full color textbook packaged together with an interactive CD-ROM. The Interactive Companion CD-ROM contains the learning objectives established by the text author for each chapter of the text. Media assets such as video and audio clips, weblinks, activities and Practice Tests are tied to these learning objectives.

The User's Guide that came with your CD-ROM explains more about how the Interactive Companion works.

TEACHING WITH THE INTERACTIVE COMPANION

You probably adopted the Interactive Companion because you knew it would add variety to your course materials, motivating students to learn. The benefits for student learning are detailed in your User's Guide, but students cannot experience these benefits if they are not using the CD-ROM to learn. This Teaching Tool will provide solid instructional ideas to help you integrate the CD into your existing course structure.

Assisting Students - Getting Started

If you have access to a computer lab, take students step-by-step through the installation process. Have students insert the CD-ROM into the CD drive and follow along as you install the program on your own computer.

If you do not have access to a computer lab, but have access to a computer and projection equipment, demonstrate the installation on your own computer. Take students through a tour of the Interactive Companion by leading them through the "Interactive Companion Help" section of the CD-ROM. Discuss topics such as navigation, the media icons, and the Media Index.

If you are teaching in a lecture class and do not have access to a computer, you can describe the installation process and what students might expect to see and do once they begin using the CD-ROM. You can recommend to students that they look at the "Interactive Companion Help" section of the CD-ROM when getting started. Part of the fun of using the interactive CD-ROM is in the exploration. Most students will enjoy learning about it on their own.

Here are suggestions for how you might incorporate the Interactive Companion into your classroom assignments.

Individual Writing Assignments

- **Using video or audio clips as a stimulus for writing.** Ask students to analyze the video or audio clips based on the text or other readings. How can they use the concepts in the course to talk about the events on the video or audio clips?

- **Have students create a journal.** For every chapter, students must write in their journal about their favorite Web site from among the Weblinks on the CD-ROM and explain why it is significant within the context of the course.

- **Use the Weblinks on the CD-ROM** as the basis for essays or reaction papers. Create assignments around Weblinks that bring current issues into course work.

Collaborative Writing Assignments

By working in groups, individual student products are shared to produce a superior group product. Not only does this cut down on the number of papers the instructor needs to grade, but it also encourages students to learn from each other.

- Set up "electronic communities" of students and assign an Internet activity from the CD-ROM to complete cooperatively. Ask them to communicate about their ideas only through e-mail so they have to express themselves clearly in writing and so there is a record of each person's contribution. As part of the assignment, have them review the transcripts of their discussions and analyze what helped them learn and what helped them produce a good final product.

Practice Tests and Activities

- Each Practice Test and Activity can be emailed to the instructor from within the Interactive Companion. Choose a few activities and Practice Tests in each chapter and have the students email you their work so you can monitor their progress in the class.
- Let students know that you will be selecting a few questions from the Practice Tests on the CD-ROM to be used in their own exams. This will encourage students to test themselves and monitor their own progress.

Research

Discuss with students how to analyze a Web site for reliability. This is a good opportunity for students to learn about becoming discriminating Web users. Ask them how they might evaluate Web resources in the context of the five traditional print evaluation criteria: accuracy, authority, objectivity, currency and coverage. Have them consider the following questions:

- Who is the creator of the site?
- What is the authority or expertise of the individual or group that created the site?
- Is there an evident bias in the site?
- Do the Web pages have many typos and grammatical mistakes that may indicate a lack of editorial oversight and questionable accuracy of content?

Encourage students to use additional references from the Interactive Companion in their term papers. Give them extra credit if they include online research in their work.

Class Presentation and Discussion

- Organize students into groups and have each group present the major points of one chapter in the book to the rest of the class. Suggest to students that they use elements from the Interactive Companion in their presentations or as part of their research to create a multimedia presentation integrating electronic and print resources.

- Use video or audio clips as a springboard for classroom debates.

Large Classroom Assignments

Assigning activities for large classes can sometimes be challenging. The activities listed for each chapter in this Teaching Tool, however, can be easily adapted in a variety of and the instructor. Students can then e-mail their results to you, or you can ask a member of each group to share their results with the class.

How to Use This Teaching Tool

The Teaching Tool will show you how to implement the Interactive Companion in your course. As you plan your syllabus and lectures each semester, look to the Teaching Tool to provide discussion starters, classroom exercises, homework, and even test questions. The Interactive Companion should not be dismissed as a student supplement that they use at their own discretion. Because it offers such a potential benefit to students, the Interactive Companion should be an integral part of your course – as important as the textbook you chose to adopt.

In each chapter of this Teaching Tool you will find teaching notes for a selection of media assets on the Interactive Companion. Not every media asset is discussed in this manual. Each entry includes:

- **Annotation.** This briefly describes the media asset being discussed. For example, it might describe the action of a video clip or the content of a Web site.
- **Learning Objective.** Describes what the student will learn by reviewing the media asset.
- **Faculty Note.** Explains the purpose for using the media asset and what particular concept the asset will address. Often, it will include a page reference to the textbook that shows where the concept is being discussed.
- **Activity.** Suggests an activity that can be done in class, for homework, or as a long-term project based on the content of the media asset.
- **Additional Resources.** These are books, articles, or other Web sites that expand on the media asset.
- **Test Question.** Multiple choice, essay, and True/False questions are provided so that you can assess students' understanding of the media asset.
- **Test Bank.** The test questions from each chapter can be found at the end of the manual, aggregated to make it easier to prepare tests.

This information will help you use the Interactive Companion more fully in your course. Good luck!

CHAPTER 1: EXCEPTIONALITY AND SPECIAL EDUCATION

Audio 1.1 Thinking it Over

Annotation: Dr. Kauffman discusses the relationship between general and special education. He highlights key issues related to what is meant by "special education"—including the unique learning needs of students with disabilities and what that means in terms of the education they should receive. Additionally, questions are raised in regard to the training of general and special educators.

Learning Objective: Articulate the purpose of special education and match learner needs to instructional options.

Faculty Note: Dr. Kauffman raises a variety of questions—many that do not have clear answers. The questions raised will help students define for themselves the purpose of education and stimulate thought related to what services are needed and how those services are best delivered. Additionally, the controversial nature of the questions prompts students to consider a variety of perspectives. Information on the definition of special education and placement options (pp. 12-18) will provide some information to start students thinking about the issues related to providing appropriate education to students with disabilities.

Activity: Have students work in groups to complete the following matrix:

Learner Characteristic	Requisite Modification	Optimal Instructional Environment	Delivery person (general or special educator, other)	Placement
Ex.: Reading 3 levels below grade level *Ex: Uses a wheelchair*	*Systematic instruction in reading* *Wheelchair access— doors, around the class/school, etc.*	*Small, homogeneous group* *Room with space to access all materials and information*	*Special educator or reading specialist* *General educator*	*Resource room or self-contained* *General education classroom*

Additional Resources: See the table on pages 16-17 of the text

Test Question: <u>Essay:</u> List and describe four things that make special education different from general education.

[*Answer*: Appropriate responses include: individualized instruction, adherence to federal guidelines, continuum of alternative placements, FAPE requirement, instruction that is systematic, structured, and explicit, specialized training, and assessment requirements (typically more frequently than general education and progress monitoring more specified).]

Weblink 1.2 Office of Special Education Programs (OSEP)

Annotation: This weblink takes students to the official site of the Office of Special Education Programs (OSEP). OSEP is part of the Office of Special Education and Rehabilitative Services (OSERS), which is one of the principal components of the U.S. Department of Education. OSEP's mission and organization focus on the free appropriate public education of children and youth with disabilities from birth through age 21. At this site, students can find information on the Individuals with Disabilities Education Act Amendments of 1997, guidelines for creating individualized education programs (IEPs), and descriptions of federal research initiatives.

Learning Objective: Explain the IEP process and identify key components related to the Amendments of 1997.

Faculty Note: The OSEP website will provide students with up-to-date and extensive information related to IDEA (pp.28-29) and the IEP process (pp.33-39). Activity I will guide students through the nuts and bolts of how to create legally sound IEPs. Activity II allows students to view commonly asked questions related to providing special education services and OSEP's responses to those questions. Although these activities highlight only part of the overall site, students will become familiar with the overall site layout and have the opportunity to take an in-depth look at one of OSEP's many roles.

Activity I: Have students click on "Guide to the Individualized Education Program" under the "What's New" section. Here, students will find information related to the IEP process. Have students create a flow chart of the IEP process. At each step, students must write a brief description of what takes place at that step.

Activity II: Have students go to the "IDEA '97" section, then click on "New Overheads on OSEP's Correspondence." Divide students into groups and assign one of the "correspondence questions" to each group. The group can then read and summarize the response. Then, bring all groups together to share the questions and answers.

Additional Resources:

  National Information Center for Children and Youth with Disabilities (NICHCY)
  P.O. Box 1492
  Washington, DC 20013
  (800) 695-0285 (Voice/TTY); (202) 884-8200 (V/TTY)
  E-mail: nichcy@aed.org
  Web: www.nichcy.org
  Technical Assistance for Parent Centers--the Alliance
  PACER Center
  4826 Chicago Avenue South
  Minneapolis, MN 55417-1098
  (888) 248-0822; (612) 827-2966; (612) 827-7770 (TTY)
  E-mail: alliance@taalliance.org

Web: www.taalliance.org

Test Question(s):

Essay. Describe the steps necessary for identifying a student for special education.

[*Answer*: Students should include information related to parent notification, testing procedures, decision–making procedures, and procedural safeguards.]

Multiple Choice. Identify the correct order of the IEP process:
>   a. evaluation, eligibility determination, IEP, services, IEP review, IEP re-eval
>   b. evaluation, eligibility determination, IEP, services, IEP re-eval, IEP review
>   c. eligibility determination, IEP, evaluation, services, IEP review, IEP re-eval
>   d. IEP, evaluation, eligibility determination, IEP re-eval, IEP review

[*Answer*: B]

Activity 1.4 Review of Key Terms

Annotation: Students are reminded of the difference between a handicap and a disability. Definitions are provided in a format similar to an electronic flashcard.

Learning Objective: Understand the instructional implications to the reduction of handicaps.

Faculty Note: The authors make a point of differentiating "disability" from "handicap" (p. 6). This activity reinforces this distinction as well as facilitates student understanding of the permanent nature of some disabilities and the instructional obligation of teachers to recognize how to help students achieve to the best of their abilities—thus, reducing the number of unnecessary handicaps in students' lives.

Activity: Create a list of handicaps that can be reduced or removed by a teacher by changing the environment or changing instruction.

Additional Resources: none

Test Question(s):

Essay. In what ways should making the distinction between "disability" and "handicap" influence teachers' instructional decisions.

[*Answer*: Teachers who understand this distinction are able to recognize things within the environment (such as physical, attitudinal, or instructional barriers) that serve as "handicaps" to the individual. Focusing upon what is in their control to change, they can work to reduce these handicaps and teach students ways to be successful despite their disability.]

Fill in the Blank.

1. _____   is the inability to do something or a diminished capacity to
                    perform in a specific way.

2. _____   is a disadvantage imposed on an individual.

[*Answer*: (1) disability; (2) handicap]

Weblink 1.4 Office of Special Education Publications

Annotation: OSEP's <u>Annual Report to Congress on the Implementation of the Individuals with Disabilities Education Act</u> for 1999 is presented. Executive summary, section by section downloads, and all data charts are provided.

Learning Objective: Collect data from home state on the identification rates across age groups and disability categories. Identify trends in identification for certain disability categories.

Faculty Note: Students will have the opportunity to use the actually 1999 report to congress to collect data on their state's identification rates. By examining the patterns in identification across disability categories, students will begin to recognize differences among the categories, such as which disability categories remain stable across age levels, which are identified early, what patterns are evident as students get older, etc.

Activity: Provide the following instructions to your students: Go the OSEP section "On line publications." Click on "21ˢᵗ Annual Report (1999)." Read the Executive summary. The summary addresses recent changes to IDEA (1997) and notes key issues related to implementation. After reviewing the summary, open "Appendix Part I: Data Tables." Using the data from these charts, create a table that includes the following data from your home state only: the total number of students with disabilities, the number of students served per age group, and the number of students served per disability category. Once you have completed your table, note any patterns in identification. Did any numbers surprise you—higher or lower than expected numbers for certain disability categories? Why do some disability categories remain fairly stable across age groups? What hypothesis do you have regarding the categories that do not remain stable?

Additional Resources: For further exploration, students can view "Appendix Part II: Data Tables" for information regarding placement in different educational environments. Students could also make comparisons between their state and surrounding states.

Test Question: <u>Essay.</u> Describe overall trends in the identification of students with disabilities. Include key factors related to the identification of certain disabilities and how that relates to identification patterns.

[*Answer:* Appropriate answers should include such things as the noted stability across disability categories that are easily identifiable such as physical disabilities or autism, increase in students identified as behavioral disordered and learning disabled as they get older, relatively low numbers of students identified as behavioral disordered compared to learning disabilities or speech/language impairments, higher numbers than expected of students identified at OHI—link to increased identification rates of ADHD, drop off of "developmentally delayed" label in some states after age 9, etc.]

Weblink 1.7 Education World

Annotation: Education World provides information to teachers on everything from curriculum to grant opportunities. Under the "special education" section, teachers (and parents) can find information on specific disabilities, advocacy organizations, assessment, assistive technology, and teacher resources. This activity guides students through an ERIC document on ADA, IDEA, and Section 504 of the Rehabilitation Act.

Learning Objective: Compare and contrast laws that protect the rights of students with disabilities and highlight implications for classroom teachers.

Faculty Note: Students often have a difficult time sorting out the legal responsibilities of special education teachers. This activity will help them make clear distinctions between three laws that pertain to students with disabilities. The article guides students through each of the sections on the table.

Activity: Compare information on ADA, IDEA, and Section 504. Go to "Education World" and click on "Special Education." Then select "Overview of ADA, IDEA, and Section 504." Using the information given, complete the table:

Information	ADA	IDEA	504
Type/Purpose			
Who is Protected?			
Responsibility to FAPE			
Funding			
Procedural Safeguards			
Evaluation/Placement			
Due Process			

Additional Resources:
- The ADA Information Line, 1-800-514-0301 (voice); 1-800-514-0383 (TDD).
- Council of Administrators of Special Education, Inc. (1991). Student access: A resource guide for educators, Section 504 of the Rehabilitation Act of 1973. Albuquerque, NM: Author.
- Council for Exceptional Children, Department of Public Policy. (1994). The rights of children with disabilities under ADA and Section 504: A comparison to IDEA. Reston, VA: Author.

- ERIC Clearinghouse on Disabilities and Gifted Education. (1992). Legal foundations 1: Section 504 of the Rehabilitation Act and the Americans with Disabilities Act. Reston, VA: Author.
- Morrissey, P. (1993). The educator's guide to the ADA. Alexandria, VA: American Vocational Association.

Test Question:

True/False. The requirement for "reasonable accommodations" in ADA is similar to the FAPE requirement of IDEA in that both address the need for specially designed instruction.

[*Answer:* True]

Activity 1.9 Understanding Roles

Annotation: Students will hear two audio clips. The first clip is of teachers and a student talking about their experiences in an inclusive class. The second clip is of an administrator describing the collaboration that ideally occurs between general and special educators working in an inclusive setting.

Learning Objective: Identify the various roles and responsibilities integral to the successful inclusion of students with disabilities in the general education setting.

Faculty Note: Students will hear first hand accounts of what teachers believe are their roles within the inclusive classroom and a statement from a student with disabilities on his experience in an inclusive class. The teachers make general and specific statements regarding their roles. Then, the administrator delineates what he believes are the responsibilities of general and special educators. The statements highlight the complexity of collaborative relationships and the ambiguity of roles within inclusive classes. This activity corresponds to the material on pages 19-22 of the text.

Activity: After listening to the statements, have students complete a chart (similar to the one below) to reflect the statements made by the teachers, student, and administrator. Students can then add ideas of their own that they believe are important to successful inclusion of students with disabilities. Finally, have the students discuss possible conflicts that may arise in the maintenance/delivery of these responsibilities and brainstorm various solutions.

	General Responsibility	**Specific Responsibilities**
Special educator		
Special General educator		

Additional Resources: none

Test Question:

Essay. You are a special education teacher who is about team-teach in a general education classroom next year. Write a letter to the general education teacher that delineates what you believe are your roles and responsibilities within his or her classroom. *hint: be as specific as possible

[*Answer:* Various responses. Appropriate responses will include the role of the IEP in instructional decision making, need for instruction that meets the needs of the student, need for clear expectations, active role within the instruction and management within the classroom, etc.]

Weblink 1.9 National Public Radio

Annotation: Laurie Block, NPR correspondent, doing a piece on "Charity" stumbles into a whole genre of children's books that graphically depict children with disabilities. In each story, the disability is projected as "God's will" and the children submissively accept this martyrdom as their role in life. Experts from the stories are read. Both audio clip and transcript are provided.

Learning Objective: Compare and contrast the portrayal of people with disabilities during the 1800s with modern day representations.

Faculty Note: The audio (along with the written transcript) is a powerful way for students to experience these children's books of the 1800s. As students listen to the stories and commentary, parallels can be drawn to today's media depiction of people, especially children, with disabilities. Striking contrasts are also apparent—from changes in language to changes in opportunity. Awareness of changing the "blessed innocents" image to "persons with capabilities" image is important for future teachers who need to recognize the individuality of children with disabilities and challenge them to maximize their potential.

Activity: Play the audio in class (or have students listen to it on their own). It is helpful to have a copy of the transcript while listening to the audio clip. Have students brainstorm (or collect) media representations of children with disabilities. Media can include current children's stories, commercials, TV shows, advertisements for organizations (Easter Seals, Shriners, etc.), public signage, movies, etc. Finally, have students decide whether the portrayal is reminiscent of the 1800s or sends a different message.

Additional Resources:
>   Rotary International (http://www.rotary.org/)
>   Shriners (http://www.shriners.com/)
>   National Easter Seals (http://www.easter-seals.org/)
>   Family Voices (http://www.familyvoices.org/)

Test Question:
Essay. In what ways to changes in language reflect changes in opportunities for children with disabilities?

[*Answer:* Various answers. Appropriate answers include reference to increased opportunities, higher expectations, and an emphasis on individual responsibility and power that have come with changing attitudes regarding disabilities.]

Audio 1.5 Trends in Litigation

Annotation: Dr. Kauffman discusses trends in litigation on placement decisions and the apparent notion that the courts and parents "favor" placement in the general education classroom over more restrictive placements. In actuality, more parents bring suit in order to get more restrictive, more individualized education. The courts favor placement decisions that are made on an individual basis and whose overriding concern is the development of an appropriate education.

Learning Objective: Understand the relationship between LRE and appropriate education.

Faculty Note: Students may often misinterpret the LRE clause to mean wholesale placement in the general education classroom. By having students see how the courts interpret LRE, students gain a greater understanding of how to make instructionally sound placement decisions.

Activity: Have students listen to the audio clip and then write several paragraphs in which they discuss why they believe that parents would seek more restrictive placements and what the responsibilities of the special educator are to the LRE clause.

Additional Resources:
- Newcomer, J. R., & Zirkel, P. A. (1999). An analysis of judicial outcomes of special education cases. Exceptional Children, 65(4), 469-480.

Test Question:
Essay. Dr. Kauffman suggests that the "appropriate education" aspect supersedes the "LRE" clause. What does that mean in terms of placement decisions? How should this be reflected in determining placement? Give specific examples for each.

[*Answer*: Various responses. Appropriate responses include the fact that IEP teams should first determine what the instructional goals and objectives are for an individual and then, they must determine how those goals can be met. Finally, teams should decide what the most supportive environment (with deference to LRE) for addressing those objectives is. Examples should be provided.]

CHAPTER 2: CURRENT TRENDS AND ISSUES

Weblink 2.2 Renaissance Group

Annotation: This web site is produced by the Renaissance Group and provides information to teachers about inclusion. Categories include: philosophy, legal requirements, teacher competencies, teacher strategies, and inclusion resources.

Learning Objective: Evaluate recommendations made by the Renaissance Group that support the adoption of full inclusion.

Faculty Note: The Renaissance Group endorses a "full inclusion" philosophy (pp.48-58). It is important for students to explore the ramifications of such a stance in terms of what supports are necessary for successful inclusion. This activity will allow students to critically examine the recommendations of the group. For further exploration of the issues, students can contrast the recommendations made by the Renaissance Group with those made on the LD OnLine site. Strategy information is provided under the "Teaching Tools" section of LD OnLine. In addition, the position statement by the National Joint Committee on Learning Disabilities on full inclusion provides information that may guide students in their response to the "potential concerns" column of the activity (http://www.ldonline.org/njcld/react_inclu.html).

Activity: Go to the "Teaching Strategies" section of the Renaissance Group web site. Have your students open the "Content/Behavior" section. Using a three-column note structure with "Recommendation" heading the first column, "Implementation Considerations" heading the second, and "Potential Concerns" heading the third, have students select at least four of the recommendations and fill them into the first column. Then, in groups, the students should determine what specific things a teacher can do to reflect each recommendation. Finally, students consider any potential concerns related to the recommendation. For example, the recommendation may so broad as to lead to different interpretations or the recommendation may be contrary to what is known to be effective for students with disabilities.

Recommendation	Implementation Consideration	Potential Concerns
• Teachers throw out the worksheets and basal reader system; they create curriculum that involves students.	• Teachers need to find out the interests of their students and incorporate that into the curriculum • Teachers should adopt a more constructivist curriculum that involves more indirect/child-centered instruction	• Child-centered curriculum may lack the structure and explicitness necessary for students with learning and behavioral disabilities to be successful • "Teacher-made" curriculum may be inadequate for successful student learning • Lack of specification as to what a "curriculum that involves all students" looks like

Additional Resources: See the Renaissance Group "Resources" section of the web site for lists of articles, books, schools, organizations, and other web sites all related to inclusion: http://www.uni.edu/coe/inclusion/resources/resources.html

Test Question: <u>Essay.</u> Dr. Christopher Kliewer makes the statement: "Inclusive education is nothing more than good teaching for all students." Given what you know about history of special education and the legal requirement for "specially designed instruction that meets the unusual needs of an exceptional student," in what ways can this statement be interpreted as true and in what ways can it be interpreted as false.

[*Answer*: Various responses. Appropriate answers should include specific examples of how good teaching equals effective teaching and therefore, the majority of students will benefit from what researchers support as effective teaching. Examples include clearly stating objectives, high levels of student engagement, repetition of concepts to mastery, and relevant and interesting content. On the other hand, what is needed for some students is not necessary for others; therefore, "good" teaching for some students might be disastrous for others. Examples could include such extremes as students who are gifted with students with mental retardation and their academic needs, or more subtle examples of students who benefit from explicit and structured instruction (i.e., students with learning disabilities) and those who benefit from open-ended, exploratory instruction.]

Audio 2.4 Standards of Learning and Exceptional Students

Annotation: In this audio clip, Dr. Kauffman describes some of the incompatibilities of the standard's movement with legal obligations to provide individualized education to students with disabilities and hyperabilities.

Learning Objective: Debate the pro's and con's of the standards movement and its effect on special education.

Faculty Note: This activity corresponds with the discussion in the text related to "standards-based" reforms (p.66). Dr. Kauffman presents a bleak picture of how the standards movement can affect special education programming. This activity will help students recognize these and other potential limitations and conflicts, while identifying potential positive effects of the movement.

Activity: Have students form debate teams (no more than 5 students per team). Half of the teams will be "pro" standards and half of the teams will be "against" standards (or "pro individualized, instructional decision-making"). Student should collect information to support their side. Each group will prepare a bulleted list of their arguments. Then have the class come together to "debate" the issues—in a point-counter point fashion.

Additional Resources:
Web sites with articles related to standards movement:
- Council for Basic Education Judging Standards in Standards-based Reform:
  http://www.c-b-e.org/articles/ipperspt.htm
- Biographies on Standards Reform:
  http://www.negp.gov/Reports/9massell.htm (see "Equity and Standards-Based Reforms")
- Grading School Reform: Complex Problem Defies Standards-Based Reform:
  http://www.pipeline.com/~rgibson/rouge_forum/grdschlref.htm
- TIMSS and Standards-Based Reforms
  http://www.ed.gov/pubs/TIMSSBrief/reforms.html
- Educating One & All: Students with Disabilities and Standards-Based Reform
  http://www.nap.edu/html/edu/

Test Question:

Essay. You are a special education teacher who is working with a general educator in a fourth grade class. Your team teacher tells you that your state is implementing a "standards test" at the end of this year; therefore, she wants to do less curriculum modification so that all students, including those with disabilities, will do well on the test. How do you respond?

[*Answer:* Answers should include acknowledgement of the importance of high standards for all students, yet the importance of the obligation to IEP requirements—specifically instructional objectives and delineated accommodations, the necessity of those modifications for the learning of your students, and the importance carefully examining each competency or skill area and making individual decision rather wholesale decisions on whether or not to modify.]

Weblink 2.2 Abecedarian Project

Annotation: Frank Porter Graham Child Development Center presents results from one of the few longitudinal research projects related to early intervention. The Abecedarian Project studied the impact of educational intervention in the lives of preschool-aged children from low-income families. The research project began in the 1970's and followed kids from birth to age 15. Results showed positive effects on cognitive and academic assessments at age 15. Design information is provided.

Learning Objective: Recognize the importance of early intervention and list components of successful early intervention programs.

Faculty Note: Many organizations state the importance of early intervention and make recommendations for practice, yet few of these recommendations have been found through research to be effective—that is, few have been empirically validated. In this activity, students will first review the design and results of the Abecedarian Project and then find other research-supported recommendations for practice. This will be a great way for future teachers to begin thinking about how to critically evaluate recommendations given by various organizations.

Activity: Students will go on an Internet scavenger hunt looking for recommendations for early intervention practices that are supported by research. Students can begin by filling in the recommendations made on the Abecedarian site and then conduct searches of early childhood agencies and organizations. After students complete the hunt, lead the students in a discussion the importance of advocating for practices that are supported by research, reasons why recommendations are made without an empirical base, and issues related to determining quality research.

Name of Organization	Recommendations	Research: Yes or No

Additional Resources:
Web sites related to early intervention:
- The National Association for the Education of Young Children
  http://www.naeyc.org/default.htm
- Defining Quality in Early Intervention
  http://idea.uoregon.edu/~ncite/documents/techrep/tech11-1.html
- Improving the Delivery of Early Intervention to Children with Disabilities from High Poverty Background
  http://www.lsi.ukans.edu/jg/Judy/highpoverty.htm
- Medicaid as Fiscal Support for Early Intervention in Missouri
  http://web.missouri.edu/~cfprwww/policy4.html
- Early Childhood Community
  http://www.isdd.indiana.edu/~ecc/proj.html

Test Question:
True/False. Effective early intervention programs have been shown by research to decrease the level of disability in some individuals.

[*Answer*: True.]

Weblink 2.6 School-to-Work Outreach Programs

Annotation: (*from the web site*) The School-to-Work Outreach Project was a nationwide, three-year project funded by the U.S. Department of Education. A primary goal of this project was to improve school-to-work opportunities for students with disabilities. Federal legislation, such as the School-to-Work Opportunities Act (STWOA) of 1994 and the Individuals with Disabilities Education Act of 1990, guide school-to-work transition efforts. The STWOA establishes a national framework within which states can create statewide school-to-work systems, and requires the inclusion and participation of youth with disabilities. The School-to-Work Outreach Project was guided by the needs of youth in their transition from school-to-work in the three core elements stated in the School-to-Work Opportunities Act of 1994:
- School-Based Learning - Instruction and experiences based on academic and occupational skills standards.
- Work-Based Learning - Workplace experience, structured training, mentoring, and apprenticeships at job sites.
- Connecting Activities - A variety of activities that build and maintain bridges between school, work, and other adult environments.

Learning Objective: Identify the components of the School-to-Work Act and examine exemplary school-to-work programs.

Faculty Note: Students will be able to read about different school-to-work programs from across the country that have been identified as exemplary. In reading the descriptions, students will gain a greater understanding of this important component of transition services. The activity corresponds with the discussion of federal initiatives found on pages 73-77 in the text.

Activity: In groups of 3 or 4, have students go to the "Exemplary Model/Practice/Strategy Profiles" section of the site (http://www.ici.coled.umn.edu/schooltowork/profiles.html). Have each group select a profile of a certain school-to-work model and evaluate the model in terms of the requirements of the School-to-Work Act. Groups can then present a summary of their profile to the other groups.

Additional Resources:
See the School-to-Works Links section of the site: (http://www.ici.coled.umn.edu/schooltowork/links.html)

Test Question:
True/False. School-to-work activities begin at age 14 and continue post-high school.

[*Answer:* FALSE]

Weblink 2.7 Early Warning, Timely Response: A Guide to Safe Schools

Annotation: "Early Warning, Timely Response: A Guide to Safe Schools" was developed by the Department of Education and the Department of Justice. It offers research-based recommendations to assist school communities in identify warning signs early and develop prevention, intervention, and crisis response plans. The guide includes sections on: characteristics of a school that is safe and responsive to all children, early warning signs, getting help for troubled children, developing a prevention and response plan, responding to crisis, and additionally resources.

Learning Objective: Develop an in-service presentation based upon the information provided in "Early Warning, Timely Response: A Guide to Safe Schools."

Faculty Note: As noted in your text (pp. 78-79), there are increasing concerns regarding the safety of schools. One reaction to recent increases in school violence and drug use is the adoption of "no tolerance" policies. Teachers who work with students with learning and behavior difficulties are increasingly faced with the challenge of understanding the relationship between disability and misbehavior. One way to support all students, but particularly students whose disabilities place them at greater risk for behavior problems, is through prevention. This activity will allow students to identify preventative practices recommended by the Department of Education.

Activity: Have students go to the OSEP web site and click on "Early Warning, Timely Response: A Guide to Safe Schools" and open the full report (either pdf or html). In groups of three to five, tell students that their charge is to create an in-service for teachers based upon the information in the document. Students will create an outline for their presentation, create overheads they may use, and design one activity that they would have the teachers do to reinforce the information they are presenting. Students may then lead other groups in their activity.

Additional Resources: none

Test Question:
Essay. In "Early Warning, Timely Response: A Guide to Safe Schools," they identify some early warning signs. List three of these and then three preventative steps a school or teacher can do to reduce the likelihood of violence.

[*Answer:* Answers can include: social withdrawal, excessive feelings of isolation and being alone, excessive feelings of rejections, being a victim of violence, low school interest, feeling of being picked on or persecuted, patterns of impulsive hitting or bullying, uncontrolled anger, history of discipline problems, drug and alcohol abuse, association with a gang, inappropriate access to guns, etc. Preventative steps include: focus on academic achievement, involve families, emphasize positive relationships, create links with the community, discuss safety issues openly, demonstrate respect to all students, create ways for students to share their feelings, offer extended day services, etc.]

Weblink 2.8 Special Education Resources on the Internet

Annotation: Special Education Resources on the Internet (SERI) is a collection of web sites of interest to those involved in fields related to Special Education. SERI is organized by disability category as well as topics related to service provision and advocacy.

Learning Objective: Synthesize a variety of position statements made by disability-advocacy groups regarding the behavioral treatment of people with disabilities.

Faculty Note: Given the diverse issues related to the discipline of students with disabilities, future educators should recognize the myriad of issues that fall under the broad heading of "behavior management." In this activity, students will have the opportunity to explore different advocacy organizations' position statements on discipline and unveil the philosophical underpinnings of the recommendations. Differences in philosophy or orientation to "misbehavior" often are reflected in the specific recommendations for practices. See if your students notice the different orientations of the organizations.

Activity: Have students search several different advocacy agency sites to collect information on discipline related issues for students with disabilities. The SERI web site will provide a gateway to a variety of sites and is organized by disability category. Students should select at least 4 different organizations and find position statements related to the discipline. Students should then compare and contrast the different stances made by the different organizations. Using a chart similar to the one below, students should record their findings and reactions. After collecting the information, students should write a summary/reaction statement regarding the discipline of students with disabilities.

Organization	Web Address	Summary of statement or position	Reaction
The ARC	http://www.thearc.org/ga/restraints_comments.html	The ARC supports the use of positive behavioral supports and are against the use of any procedures that may cause physiological or psychological harm or are dehumanizing	I think…

Additional Resources: Various web sites.

Test Question:
True/False. Students with disabilities are required by law to follow the same discipline rules as student without disabilities.

[*Answer*: False]

Activity 2.15 Review of Key Terms

Annotation: Terms and definitions for "mandatory sentencing" and "manifestation determination" are reviewed.

Learning Objective: Understand the background and legal history of manifestation determination and determine procedures for making manifestation determinations.

Faculty Note: One of the most difficult concepts related to discipline and students with disabilities is the notion of "manifestation determination." In this activity students with learn background information and specific policy procedures for making manifestation determinations. To follow up this activity, you could provide students with case studies of student behaviors and then have them apply the guidelines when making manifestation determinations. Students are introduced to the concept of manifestations determination on page 80 of the text.

Activity: Students will develop a question and answer guide for administrators and teachers regarding manifestation determination. Students should write 7-10 questions commonly asked and then write the response to those questions. Send to students to the following sites to collect data on manifestation determinations (alternatively, students can conduct their own search by using a search engine and the term "manifestation determination"):

- Oregon site on manifestation determinations:
  http://www.ode.state.or.us/sped/spedlegal/discipline/manifestation.htm.
- Vermont's Special Education Regulations:
  http://www.state.vt.us/educ/sped/4313-1.htm
- The Special Ed Advocate:
  http://www.wrightslaw.com/law/code_regs/discipline.html
- Discipline and the reauthorized IDEA
  http://www.keepschoolssafe.org/reauth.htm
- Manifestation Determination Review:
  http://www.cesa7.k12.wi.us/sped/1999spedforms/I-18.htm

Additional Resources:
(For the follow-up activity) Resources that include cases studies:

       Managing Classroom Behavior: A Reflective Case Based Approach, 2/e
       James M. Kauffman, University of Virginia
       Mark P. Mostert, Moorhead State University
       Stanley C. Trent, University of Virginia
       Daniel P. Hallahan, University of Virginia
       © 1998 / ISBN: 0-205-27460-9

       Classroom Management for Secondary Teachers: 5/e
       Emmer, Edmund
       Evertson, Carolyn
       Worsham, Murray
       © 2000 / ISBN: 0-205-30837-6

Test Question:

Multiple Choice. If the IEP team determines that a student's misbehavior is NOT related to his or her disability, then:

    a. Traditional discipline procedures established for students without disabilities are followed.

    b. A functional behavioral analysis must be conducted.

    c. The student is released from his or her IEP.

    d. The student may be disciplined using traditional discipline procedures, but is still ensured FAPE.

[*Answer:* D]

Activity 2.16 Concept Check

Annotation: Matching activity where students match 12 terms from the chapter to their definitions.

Learning Objective: Link key terms with appropriate section of the text.

Faculty Note: This activity will help students prepare for their exam. Students will use the twelve terms as a guide and then reference the page numbers.

Activity: First, students should complete the matching activity. Then, correct any incorrect answers. After they have correctly matched all 12 terms, they should reference the page in their text that corresponds with the term. This will serve as a study guide for students as they prepare for the exam.

Additional Resources: none

Test Question:

Essay. Write a several paragraph essay in which you summarize current trends and issues in special education. Be sure to include the following terms: normalization, full inclusion, continuum of alternative placements, disability rights movement, access to general education curriculum, and manifestation determination.

[*Answer:* Various responses.]

CHAPTER 3: MULTICULTURAL AND BILINGUAL ASPECTS OF SPECIAL EDUCATION

Audio 3.1 Thinking It Over

Annotation: Dr. Kauffman discusses the distinction between deviance and difference and the implications each has for what we tolerate and teach.

Learning Objective: To become aware of the number of messages that teach children to be tolerant of violence and aggression.

Faculty Note: In Dr. Kauffman's discussion of difference and deviance, he highlights the fact that American society has a tendency to tolerate the deviant behaviors of violence and aggression. In this activity, students will explore the importance of recognizing deviant behaviors and labeling them as such in order to prevent harmful cycles. Doing this activity at the start of the chapter will establish a framework for discussing differences and being able to identify which differences are acceptable within our schools and communities and which are not. Additionally, students will begin to explore the relationship between cultural values and attitudes and actions.

Activity: Have students explore the "tolerance" of aggression and violence within our society. Break the students into small groups. Each groups is responsible creating a list of specific examples that reinforce the notion that aggression and violence are either acceptable "differences" or unacceptable "deviances." Messages come from all kinds of places—TV, movies, music, popular jokes, commercials, print ads, fiction, news, and even some laws. After the groups have created their lists, bring the class back together to discuss some proactive ways in which this "tolerance" message can be combated.

Additional Resources: none

Test Question:
True/False. The identification of deviant behaviors can contribute to the reduction of undesired outcomes such as dropping out of school, incarceration, and being in abusive relationships.

[*Answer:* True]

Weblink 3.1 The Urban Institute

Annotation: The Urban Institute is a nonprofit policy research organization established in Washington, D.C., in 1968. The web site contains information about current urban issues, their research and publications, and ways to become involved in the issues.

Learning Objective: Become aware of a current issue related to urban welfare.

Faculty Note: This web site provides non-partisan information on a range of issues relating to urban concerns. Student who may be unfamiliar with the issues can gather information on a range of issue that affect some of the students they will one day serve.

Activity: Send your students to the Urban Institute site and have them select a topic of their choice. Students should read the background information about the issue and then write a journal reaction to the issue. Some questions you could have your students respond to in their journals would be: In what ways was the information new to you? How did you feel about the issue and the UI stance on the topic? What can teachers do to address this issue?

Additional Resources: none

Test Question:
True/False. The Urban Institute reports on issues relating to life in the inner cities.

[*Answer:* False]

Weblink 3.2 Center for Research on Education, Diversity, & Excellence

Annotation: This web site provides the Center for Research on Education, Diversity, and Excellence's five standards for effective pedagogy. The five standards are: (1) joint productive activity, (2) language development, (3) contextualization, (4) challenging activities, and (5) instructional conversation. Descriptions and examples for each are given.

Learning Objective: Students will apply the five standards for effective pedagogy.

Faculty Note: Often, teachers are provided with recommendations for practice and yet are never challenged to operationalize those recommendations. This activity will help students develop classroom practices that will reflect the 5 standards established by CREDE. The information the student's will explore on the site corresponds to the instructional issues raised in the text on pages 103-107.

Activity: Divide your students into groups based upon what age and subject (or population) they are interested in teaching. Within their age and subject groups, students will develop specific classroom practices that reflect the 5 standards.

Additional Resources: none

Test Question:
True/False. Contextualization refers to the process of making abstractions concrete and relevant to students' lives.

[*Answer:* True]

Weblink 3.3 National Academy Press

Annotation: This site contains the report from the National Academy Press summarizing their workshop on "Cultural Diversity and Early Education." Areas included in the report are: cultural context of learning, cultural diversity at home, what children bring to school, implications for early education, and directions for research.

Learning Objective: Understand key issues related to the education of children from diverse backgrounds.

Faculty Note: It is essential for teachers to recognize the factors that contribute to success in schools. Further, effective teachers recognize which variables are within their control and can influence student achievement. During this activity, students will have the opportunity to explore issues related to the education of students from diverse backgrounds. While understanding the variables that are "outside of their control," students will hone in on specific recommendations for practice that are within their control.

Activity: Read the consensus statement on cultural diversity and then write a letter to parents discussing what steps you will take in your classroom to support their child.

Additional Resources:
- **National Association for the Education of Young Children, 1989.** The Anti-bias Curriculum: Tools for Empowering Young Children. Washington, D.C.: National Association for the Education of Young Children.
- **National Association for Family Day Care, 1990.** Helping Children Love Themselves and Others: A Professional Handbook for Family Day Care Providers. Washington, D.C.: National Association for Family Day Care.
- **National Association of State Boards of Education, 1988.** Right from the Start: The Report of the NASBE Task Force on Early Childhood Education. Alexandria, Va.: National Association of State Boards of Education.
- **National Research Council, 1992.** Assessing Evaluation Studies: The Case of Bilingual Education Strategies. Panel to Review Evaluation Studies of Bilingual Education, Committee on National Statistics. Washington, D.C.: National Academy Press.

Test Question:
Essay. In what ways to children's home experiences, particularly pre-school years, have on their performance in school. Be sure to identify key factors related to school success or failure. Then state 3 things schools can do to ameliorate some of these differences.

[*Answer:* Answers should include reference to research that has demonstrated that students who lack exposure to language, literacy, and numeracy in the pre-school years, are at a deficit when they begin school. Solutions include: increased parent involvement through early intervention programs, provide effective instruction/experiences in the deficit areas, and having programs that reflect the culture of the students and families.]

Activity 3.5 Review of Key Terms

Annotation: Definitions are provided for the following terms: multicultural education, macroculture, microculture, ethnic group, and exceptionality group.

Learning Objective: Reinforce the concepts of micro- and macro-culture and identify specific examples of each.

Faculty Note: Unfortunately, some people limit their definition of diversity to ethnic or linguistic differences. Yet, the text refers to many differences (p. 92). These differences can be framed in light of micro- and macro-cultural differences. In this activity students will explore their own notions of diversity and identify how differences can affect student achievement.

Activity: Have students review the key terms for this section (Activity 3.5). Then, Using Bank's (1994) six components of culture, have students create a list of student behaviors/traits that fall into each category. Students should write examples of teaching behaviors or condition that could increases chance of failure and ways that teachers could increase chance of success for each of their examples.

Category	Examples of Behaviors/Traits	Ways in which learning could be hindered	Ways to support learning
• Values and Behavioral Styles • Languages and dialects • Nonverbal communication • Awareness of one's cultural distinctiveness • Frames of reference • Identification			

Additional Resources: none

Test Question:
Essay. List and provide examples of Bank's six components of culture.

[*Answer:* Bank's six components are: values and behavioral styles, language and dialects, nonverbal communication, awareness of one's cultural distinctiveness, frames of reference, and identification. Examples will vary.]

Weblink 3.6 National Clearinghouse for Bilingual Education

Annotation: The National Clearinghouse for Bilingual Education (NCBE) is funded by the U.S. Department of Education's Office of Bilingual Education and Minority Languages Affairs (OBEMLA). NCBE's charges is to collect, analyze, and disseminate information relating to the effective education of linguistically and culturally diverse learners in the U.S. The section highlighted for this activity is an essay written by an ESL educator regarding his experience growing up as a second language learner.

Learning Objective: Understand the perspective of a U.S. Hispanic educator who seeks to find a balance between his heritage and U.S. culture.

Faculty Note: First hand accounts can be a powerful way to introduce to students to the complex issues associated with instructing students from diverse backgrounds. Joel Gomez's article touches upon some of the issues inherent to the "dilemma of difference" discussed in the text on pages 103-104.

Activity: Go to the essay, "On Being An-American," by Joel Gomez: (http://www.ncbe.gwu.edu/classroom/voices/gomez.htm or begin at the home page, click on "In the classroom," and then open "Voices in the Field" to find his essay. Have students read the essay and then write a response to it. Journal prompts: How did you feel after reading Joel's essay? Do you agree with Joel? Do you think that Joel's viewpoint is different from many other Hispanics? What about immigrants from other backgrounds? If you had been one of Joel's teachers, what are some things you could have done to make his experience different?

Additional Resources: none

Test Question:
Essay. Teachers seeking to provide effective instruction for students with disabilities can face the "dilemma of difference" as described by Minow (1985). What instructional questions result from this situation?

[*Answer:* Answers should include the conflict the occurs in trying to treat all students the same and yet, recognizing and addressing differences.]

Weblink 3.9 Appropriate Services?

Annotation: Culturally and Linguistically Appropriate Services (CLAS) is a federally-funded collaborative effort of the University of Illinois at Urbana-Champaign, The Council for Exceptional Children, the University of Wisconsin-Milwaukee, the ERIC Clearinghouse on Elementary and Early Childhood Education, and the ERIC Clearinghouse on Disabilities and Gifted Education. CLAS evaluates and recommends materials for students from linguistic and culturally different backgrounds. The section highlighted in this activity is about understanding how a person's background influences his or her educational experience.

Learning Objective: Explore own unique culture and how it relates to personal learning.

Faculty Note: One way to have students begin thinking about tolerance and acceptance (p. 107) is to investigate their own culture and explore the ways in which their beliefs, values, and customs influenced their education. Personal experience with others of different backgrounds and the opportunity to "hear their story" should stimulate students to think about how such differences can be supported within schools.

Activity: Have students go to the section of CLAS on selecting classroom materials (http://www.clas.uiuc.edu/suggestions.html) and then click on the ERIC Digest articles (http://ericeece.org/pubs/digests/1999/santos99.html). Students should read the article and then write a reflection statement in which they discuss the "culture" of their family and community growing up. Students can look to the "Get to Know Yourself" section for guidance. After students have explored their own cultures, bring the class together to talk about the cultural differences within the group.

Additional Resources:
- Banks, J. (1998). The lives and values of researchers: Implications for educating citizens in a multicultural society. Educational Researcher, 27(7), 4-17.
- Lynch, E. W., & Hanson, M. J. (Eds.). (1998). Developing cross-cultural competence: A guide for working with children and their families (2nd ed.). Baltimore, MD: Paul Brookes.
- CLAS resource page: http://www.clas.uiuc.edu/links.html

Test Question:

<u>Essay.</u> Describe four different things teachers should look for when evaluating linguistically and culturally appropriate materials.

[*Answer:* Answers should include: consideration of the students—language, style, and dialect; limitations—do strengths outweigh limitations?; possible adaptations; reflection of the community; cost, time, and expenses; etc.]

CHAPTER 4: MENTAL RETARDATION

Activity 4.2 How Would You Categorize/Define Molly?

Annotation: On pages 140-141 of the text, students will read about Molly, a fifth graders with mental retardation who is included in the general education classroom. The narrative describes the parents' efforts to receive services for Molly, examples of Molly within the class, and details on her abilities.

Learning Objective: Understand how definitions relate to identification and to conceptualization of a disability.

Faculty Note: Students will read in the text about the different opinions regarding the definition of mental retardation (pp. 124-125). It is important that students understand that changes in accepted definitions could lead to differences in identification rates and services students receive. In this activity, students can use the case of Molly to discuss how the application of the AAMR definition, APA definition, or the Greenspan definition could result in different services or support for Molly.

Activity: After students respond to the questions within the activity, have them discuss how different perspectives of disability influence the definition and how different definitions can possible result in different educational goals and placements.

Additional Resources: none

Test Question:
Essay. Professionals have begun to recognize the limitations of using an IQ score as the sole criterion for the identification of mental retardation. What are some of the limitations of IQ and what additional information is sought when making these determinations?

[*Answer:* Limitations of IQ scores include: lack of consideration of adaptive skills, lack of stability if IQ scores over time and among tests, and lack of relationship between IQ scores and educational programming. Students should discuss the importance of collecting data on adaptive and functional skills.]

Weblink 4.1 The ARC of the US

Annotation: This is the official web site for ARC, a national organization that advocates for people with mental retardation. The web site includes information on legal issues, current affairs, local organizations, reference materials, position statements, and conventions. The section explored in this activity are the ARC's position statements.

Learning Objective: Explore official position statements of the largest advocacy organization for the rights of people with mental retardation.

Faculty Note: Advocacy organizations (many that were spearheaded by parents and families) play a large role within special education. Many parents of children with disabilities are members of advocacy organizations and therefore, receive information from such groups. It is important to be familiar with these organizations and their philosophical orientations. By having students read the position statements, they can gain a greater understanding of the orientation of such groups and insight into the expectations of many families.

Activity: Have students go to the "Position Statements" section of the ARC web site. Students should select one statement, read it, and then write a response to that statement. Encourage students to be honest in their responses: How did you feel when reading the statement? What concerns do you have in regard to the position? Was there any information that was new to you? What was surprising? Was the perspective inspiring or daunting?

Additional Resources: none

Test Question:
True/False. The Arc has developed position statements addressing various issues related to rights, treatment, services and programs for children and adults with mental retardation and their families to be used to influence public policy, guide media, and inform members of the community.

[*Answer:* True]

Weblink 4.4 President's Message

Annotation: The PCMR is the President's Committee on Mental Retardation. This site includes information on the mission of the committee, history of the committee, publications, and links to state and national resources. In this activity, students will read one document under the publications section.

Learning Objective: Understand the history of service delivery for people with mental retardation and the relationship between changing views and increased opportunities.

Faculty Note: "Speaking Up-Speaking Out" will provides definitions and prevalence figures of mental retardation as well as highlight issues related to current legislation, self-advocacy, and self-determination. The document goes into detail regarding services and support for students with mental retardation is will serve as great reference to share with families and colleagues.

Activity: Have students go to the "Publications" section and select, "With a little help from my friends." Under that section, have students read the first report, "Speaking Up-Speaking Out." Students should determine what kinds of supports are advocated and then determine if these supports are typically provided for students with mental retardation.

Additional Resources:
Other publications are available at: http://www.acf.dhhs.gov/programs/pcmr/public.htm or can be ordered directly by FAX from the Government Printing Office Warehouse, FAX number 301-317-5897.

Test Question:
Essay. Describe the differences among "the era of institutionalization," "era of deinstitutionalization," and the "era of community." Include the following categories in your response: objectives, priorities, who is being served, service planning, and setting.

[*Answer:* Students should highlight the changes in how persons with mental retardation are viewed (from patient to client to citizen), where they received services (facility to continuum of options to selection of supports priority over placement decision), who controls the decisions (professional to team to individual), etc.]

Weblink 4.5 Genetic Discrimination

Annotation: This link will take you to a page on the ARC site regarding genetic discrimination. The article will define genetic discrimination and discuss legal protections afforded under ADA, while noting the limitations to the legal protections.

Learning Objective: Learn what genetic discrimination is and how it affects the lives of people with presumed or actual genetic differences.

Faculty Note: After students read about the Human Genome Project in their text on page 134, this activity will extend their thinking about issues related to potential drawbacks to gene therapy. In this activity, students will read the ARC's position on genetic discrimination and therefore, gain a greater understanding of the relationship between gene research and the ethical ramifications of this work.

Activity: Go to the ARC's frequently asked questions page (http://www.thearc.org/faqs.htm). Then, scroll down to the Mental Retardation section and select "Facts about Genetic Discrimination." (Alternatively, the Weblink 4.5 button will take students directly to the page.) Students should read the statement and then have group discussion using the discussion starter: "Do you believe that insurance companies have the right to discriminate against people with actual or presumed genetic differences? Why or why not?"

Additional Resources:
Go to http://www.thearc.org/faqs.htm and scroll down to Human Genome Project Reports for detailed information from the field.

Test Question:
Multiple choice. Genetic discrimination is defined as
- a. certain genes infected or damaged due to heredity.
- b. certain genes "at risk" and susceptible to environmental hazards.
- c. differential treatment of individuals based on actual or presumed genetic differences.
- d. differential treatment of individuals who are more likely to be responsive to gene therapy.

[*Answer:* C]

Weblink 4.6 TASH

Annotation: (*from the web site*) "TASH is an international association of people with disabilities, their family members, other advocates, and professionals fighting for a society in which inclusion of all people in all aspects of society is the norm. TASH is an organization of members concerned with human dignity, civil rights, education, and independence for all individuals with disabilities." The web site contains information about membership, actions, news, and their resolutions.

Learning Objective: Read the TASH resolution regarding the continuum of services and make connections to practices that would reflect their recommendations.

Faculty Note: This activity relates to the information on service delivery models discussed in the text on pages 144-145. Students should carefully consider the implications of this statement on the educational services students with severe mental retardation will receive. In this activity, students will have the opportunity to reconsider the LRE requirement in comparison to TASH's recommendations.

Activity: Go to the TASH site. Under "TASH Resolutions," click on "Resolution on the Redefinition of a Continuum of Services." Read TASH's statement and write about the implications of these goals for students with mental retardation. In what ways might their notion of LRE be restrictive for this population of students?

Additional Resources: none

Test Question:
Essay. Pretend you are a parent of a child with mental retardation. Write a statement on what you goals— educational and social you have for your child. Include factors relating to intellectual, skill, and social growth opportunities.

[*Answer:* Responses will vary.]

Weblink 4.7 Facts about MR

Annotation: This article is from the ARC web site. It includes information on the assessment and identification of people with mental retardation.

Learning Objective: Learn the procedures for the assessment of mental retardation and common characteristics of MR.

Faculty Note: Many teachers are unaware of the assessment procedures for determining mental retardation. For this activity, students will create an information sheet on characteristics of people with MR and assessment procedures. Students can begin a notebook that they will fill as they move through the different disability categories. The final notebook would serve as a great reference as they begin their teaching.

Activity: Using the information from the web site, have students create a fact sheet that highlights the assessment procedures and typical characteristics.

Additional Resources: none

Test Question(s):
True/False. IQ scores are socially constructed and therefore, are not longer used in the identification of mental retardation.

[*Answer:* False]

True/False. Research has shown that IQ scores can be influenced through early intervention and appropriate education.

[*Answer:* True]

Weblink 4.8 Assumptions

Annotation: This link takes you to the AAMR fact sheet on mental retardation. It provides a definition of mental retardation and outline four assumptions essential to the application of the definition.

Learning Objective: Examine the AAMR assumptions and discuss the relationship between the assumptions and practice.

Faculty Note: Students should refer to their books for information on assessment (p. 135), adaptive skills (p. 136), and early intervention (p. 145-147) when completing the activity. This activity should help students become aware of the conflicts that occur between advocated best practice and actual practice. Have students consider the implications associated with implementation of "best practice."

Activity: Read the "Four Assumptions Essential to the Application of the Definition." Have students work in pairs to answer the following questions: (1) What are the challenges of applying the first assumption to standardized tests? (2) Do typical tests of adaptive functioning meet this requirement? (3) In what ways can adaptive strengths be measure? Are they currently in common practice? (4) Which practices tend to lead to improved outcomes for people with MR? Students should use their books and the web to respond to these questions.

Additional Resources:
- For a list of articles on adaptive behavior scales:
  http://home.att.net/~gfgc/adapbeh.htm
- Adaptive Behavior Inventory for Children:
  http://www.psychcorp.com/catalogs/paipc/psy125bpri.htm
- Vineland Adaptive Behavior Scale:
  http://www.agsnet.com/Bibliography/VINELANDbio.html
- California Adaptive Behavior Scale (FAQ):
  http://www.planetpress.org/cfaq~1.htm
- Comparisons of Adaptive and Maladaptive Scales:
  http://www.isd.net/bhill/compare.htm

Test Question:
True/False. Since adaptive behaviors are largely developmental, it is possible to describe a person's adaptive behavior as an age-equivalent score.

[*Answer:* True]

Audio 4.4 Lilly's Education and Audio 4.5 Lee's Education

Annotation: In each audio clip, students will hear the students', Lilly and Lee's, teachers talking about the educational goals for each student. Lilly's teacher discusses the role of peer tutoring in meeting Lilly's goals of attending and communicating. Lee's teacher discusses the use of the community to support Lee's functional curricular goals.

Learning Objective: Recognize the range of skills and goals students with mental retardation may have.

Faculty Note: When considering educational options for students with mental retardation (pp. 138-144), it is helpful for students to look at specific cases that highlight the need for curricular goals. In this activity, students will hear first hand accounts from two teachers of students with mental retardation. Students will compare and contrast the educational programs of these two different students.

Activity: Have students listen to the audio recording of Lilly and Lee's education. Then have the student break up into small groups to discuss the following questions: (1) What are the benefits, as described by the teacher for Lilly and her classmates? (2) What role should academic benefits have in her education? What about social? (3) How do Lilly and Lee's programs differ? Are similar? (4) Do you think Lilly and Lee have the same goals? (5) In what way does age influence the curricular goals? Do you think that Lilly and Lee are the same age? Why or why not?

Additional Resources: none

Test Question:
Multiple Choice. Functional academics refers to
    a. academics that can be directly linked independent functioning
    b. academics that lead to a job as a laborer
    c. academics that support students as they move to postsecondary schooling
    d. the development of skills that involve gross motor skills

[*Answer:* A]

Video 4.3 Carlyn's Teacher

Annotation: Carlyn's teacher discusses Carlyn's educational goals and progress. Goals include eating and drinking and motor planning activities.

Learning Objective: Identify educational goals of a young girl with mental retardation.

Faculty Note: Students can refer to Table 4.3 "Examples of Curriculum Activities across the School Years for Domestic, Community Living, Leisure, and Vocational Skills" when working on this activity. Students will get a clear picture from listening to Carlyn's teacher and watching Carlyn at school of what her educational program includes.

Activity: Watch the video and then see if you can list the unique educational goals of Carlyn? Given what you know from the text about the goals for people with MR, what other goals might Carlyn have?

Additional Resources: Text pages 139-144. Table on page 149.

Test Question:
Short Answer. Write three domain goal areas that a person with MR might have. Under each domain, write two specific goals.

[Answer: Possible domain categories include: academic, domestic, leisure, self-help, community living, and vocational skills. Specific goals will vary but should be operationalized and measurable.]

Audio 4.6 Important Treatment Innovations

Annotation: Dr. Hallahan describes what he believes is the most important treatment innovation for people with mental retardation in the past twenty years—supported, competitive employment.

Learning Objective: Learn about supported, competitive employment opportunities within your community.

Faculty Note: This activity will raise awareness of job opportunities for people with mental retardation within your community. This activity corresponds with the discussion of employment options on pages 148-151 in the text.

Activity: Have student locate job options for people with mental retardation within your community. Have them categorize the options as supportive, competitive employment or sheltered workshop. Additionally, see if students can name places where they have noticed employees with disabilities working. Students should compare notes and then as a class rate the level of support your community has for employment options for people with disabilities.

Additional Resources:

Test Question:
True/False. Supported employment is a workplace where adults who are disabled earn at least minimum wage and receive ongoing assistance from a specialist or job coach.

[*Answer:* True]

CHAPTER 5: LEARNING DISABILITIES

Video 5.1 Jamaal

Annotation: This video includes excerpts from interviews with Jamaal's mother and teacher as well as shows Jamaal at school working with his teacher during a Direct Instruction lesson.

Learning Objective: Link skills and skill-deficits with appropriate program supports.

Faculty Note: The focus of the video is Jamaal's teacher describing his academic needs and skills. Students will have the opportunity to not only hear the teacher catalogue these skills but also see Jamaal "in action." After viewing the clip, students may have questions about Direct Instruction, the instructional technique Jamaal's teacher was employing. Some information about DI is provided in the text on pages 184-185.

Activity: Have students watch the video clip of Jamaal and the interviews with his mother and teacher. As they watch the video, tell them to keep track of the skills and skill-deficits of Jamaal. Have students consider the following question: Does it sound like Jamaal is getting the instructional support he needs? Have students chart the skills and skill-deficits and match them with program considerations.

Skills or Skill Deficits	Program Considerations
Skills:	
Skill-deficits:	

Additional Resources:
- Hot Topics in Direct Instruction: http://users.sgi.net/~cokids/hot_topic_direct_instr.htm
  (If students research these topics on DI, encourage them to write a response.)
- The Association for Direct Instruction: http://darkwing.uoregon.edu/~adiep/
- What is Direct Instruction: http://www.advantage-schools.com/home/di.htm
- National Center for Policy Analysis: http://www.ncpa.org/pi/edu/pd051299e.html

Test Question:
Short Answer. List four components of Direct Instruction.

[*Answer:* Answers can include: based on task analysis, systematic, fast-paced, drill and practice, scripted, hand signals for prompts, choral responding, and immediate corrective feedback.]

Weblink 5.1 LD OnLine

Annotation: Dr. Hallahan discusses his concerns related to the instructional focus, or lack there of, in special education—particularly for students with learning disabilities.

Learning Objective: Consider the role of instruction in the educational programming of students with learning disabilities.

Faculty Note: Dr. Hallahan's essay corresponds to the text discussion of educational considerations on pages 181-185. Students are challenged to consider the role of instruction and how it can be at odds with current political agenda.

Activity: Go to the "First Person" section, then click on "Previous Installments" at the bottom of the screen. Open Dan Hallahan's article "We Need More Intensive Instruction." Have the students read the article and then, in groups of 3-4, consider the following questions: What are the purposes of education—academic, social, moral, political? After considering the various purposes, what should teachers' goals be for students and how are those goals best met? Does your group agree with Hallahan on the issues related to collaboration? Why or why not? Finally, have each student write a mission statement for themselves as future teachers. Students should include what goals they are committed to for their students.

Additional Resources: none

Test Question:
Short Answer. Dr. Hallahan, in his article "We Need More Intensive Instruction," discusses some of the challenges to effective collaboration. List 3 challenges to collaboration.

[*Answer:* Challenges include majority of time spent on consulting rather than teaching, effectiveness of instruction diminished due to large numbers of students, difficulties in establishing a mutually supportive relationship, outcome measures for students with LD can be disappointing.]

Weblink 5.2 LDA

Annotation: Learning Disabilities Association is a non-profit organizations that advocates for the rights people with learning disabilities. Their web site contains information about their mission, resources, alerts and bulletins, fact sheets, and membership opportunities.

Learning Objective: Compare and contrast statements regarding inclusion by various organizations that promote the welfare of people with disabilities.

Faculty Note: By having students compare the various position statements, they see a variety of perspectives regarding inclusion issues. It will be important to lead students to a careful examination of each of the statements, considering potential instructional ramifications. Discuss with students why there are these differences and what each group may have to gain by their position.

Activity: Have students go to the LDA web site (http://www.LDAAmerica.org/) and read their position statement on inclusion. How does it differ with the Renaissance Group (Weblink 2.2) and LD Online (Weblink 5.1)?

Organization	Statement on Inclusion	Differences among the groups
Learning Disabilities Association		
Renaissance Group		
LD Online		

Additional Resources:
- Renaissance Group: http://www.uni.edu/coe/inclusion/philosophy/index.html
- LD Online: http://www.ldonline.org/

Test Question:
Essay. Discuss the legal conflict that can occur between the provision of an appropriate education and LRE as stated by LDA.

[*Answer:* LDA believes that decisions regarding educational placement of students with learning disabilities must be based first on the needs of each individual student and second on the legislative requirement for LRE.]

Weblink 5.5 LD Resources

Annotation: LD Resources provides information for people with learning disabilities. The site publishes an electronic newsletter, categorizes links under relevant headings, and provides information on conferences and workshops.

Learning Objective: Develop strategies for teaching stress reduction as a part of a transition plan for students with learning disabilities.

Faculty Note: The section in the text on transition (pp. 190-191) outlines some of the factors that lead to successful postsecondary outcomes for students with learning disabilities. In this activity, students will read about the particular difficulties people with learning difficulties have with dealing with stress. The article provides a good stimulus for talking about stress-reduction strategies that secondary teachers can employ as part of the transition program.

Activity: Go to the LD Resources web site and click on "Education." Then have students read "Stress and students with learning disabilities." After reading the article, brainstorm ways in which teachers can teach students stress reduction techniques to assist in the successful transition to post-school life.

Additional Resources: none

Test Question:
<u>True/False.</u> Students with learning disabilities tend to lack appropriate coping strategies for dealing with stress.

[*Answer:* True]

Activity 5.12 Test Your Understanding

Annotation: In this multiple-choice activity, students match specific types of tests (e.g., CBA, IRI, Weschler Individual Achievement Test) to one of the 4 general categories of tests—standardized, formative, informal teacher, or authentic.

Learning Objective: Gain a greater understanding of the various types of tests and their purpose.

Faculty Note: This activity will help students become aware of a variety of assessment measures and have them begin thinking about specific applications of them. By exploring the purpose of each test, students will begin thinking about the role of assessment in instructional planning.

Activity: Have students complete the multiple-choice quiz and then, using their text and/or the Internet, find descriptions and examples for each of the tests. Under the "purpose" heading, have student write down when teachers would use this test (e.g., before, during, or after instruction), where it would be implemented (e.g., with a specialist, one-on-one, large group), and why would teachers use this assessment (i.e, What information would this type of test yield? What instructional purpose will it serve?).

Test	Description and Examples	Purpose (When, where, and why would you use this type of test?)
Standardized		
Formative		
Teacher-made		
Authentic		

Additional Resources: Various sites on the Internet. Key words include: assessment, standardized tests, formative evaluations, informal reading inventories, error analysis, portfolio assessments, and specific names of standardized tests.

Test Question:
Multiple Choice. Which of the following assessments is NOT and example of authentic assessment:
     a. Essay
     b. Portfolio
     c. Experiments and their results
     d. Informal Reading Inventory

[*Answer:* D]

Audio 5.1 Direct Instruction vs. Whole Language

Annotation: Dr. Hallahan discusses the controversy surrounding the use of Direct Instruction and the application of Whole Language principles for the reading instruction of students with learning disabilities.

Learning Objective: Identify the key components of instructional programs that incorporate Direct Instruction and those that endorse Whole Language principles.

Faculty Note: Dr. Hallahan's comments direct students to the section of the text on reading problems (p. 175). If students are not familiar with the concept of phonemic awareness, you should have them read the article by Snider listed in the additional resources.

Activity: Have students listen to the clip by Dr. Hallahan. Then, have students read the article "Why innovations come and go—and mostly go: The case of whole language" by Stephen Stall. Discuss in class the problems with educational trends and see if your students can come up with ways to be resistant to "fads."

Additional Resources:
- Stahl, S. A. (1999). Why innovations come and go (and mostly go): The case of whole language. Educational Researchers, 28(8), 13-22.
- Snider, V. E. (1997). The relationship between phonemic awareness and later reading achievement. Journal of Educational Research, 90(4), 203-211.

Test Question:
True/False. Direct Instruction, shown by extensive research to bring about long-term academic gains, is among the most popular way to teach students with learning disabilities to read.

[*Answer:* False]

Video 5.2 Bridget

Annotation: Bridget's teacher discusses some of the skills that Bridget has that allow her to be successful in her mainstream classes. Emphasis is on the social and advocacy skills that are critical to gaining necessary academic support.

Learning Objective: Identify the important role that social skills and self-advocacy play in being successful in school and post-school.

Faculty Note: Pre-service teachers may focus upon the academic needs of student with learning disabilities to the neglect of important social and advocacy goals that are equally important for success in mainstream classes and society. This activity highlights some goals that should be a part of transition planning for students with learning disabilities.

Activity: Have students view the video clip of Bridget, then list the skills the help Bridget be successful in her mainstream class. Many students with learning disabilities lack these essential "social and advocacy skills." Lead the class in a discussion that uses the following question as a discussion starter: What are some ways teachers can teacher and promote such self-determination?

Additional Resources:
- Wehmeyer, M. L., Agran, M., Hughes, C. (1998). Teaching self-determination to students with disabilities. Baltimore: Brookes.

Test Question:
Essay. Define self-determination and discuss how it relates to students with learning disabilities.

[*Answer:* Self-determination involves knowing what one wants and understanding what is necessary to bring it about. Students with disabilities typically lack these skills and must be explicitly taught them. Self-determination becomes more important as students get older and need to advocate for themselves more frequently. Self-determination has recently be recognized as one the overriding goals of transition programming.]

Activity 5.25 Steve-Difficulties in school; Success in the workplace

Annotation: This activity features two video clips of Steve. In the first video, Steve discusses his negative experiences in school. In the second clip, Steve discusses how he found success in the workplace and what strengths he works from to make it a success.

Learning Objective: Explore the factors that lead to positive experiences in school and identify activities that help foster successful transitions to postsecondary work or schooling

Faculty Note: In this activity, students will think about what teachers can do to create positive learning experiences while in school and how they can build on strengths to create programs that lead to successful postsecondary experiences. A description of postsecondary programming is found in the text on pages 192-193.

Activity: First, have the students watch the first clip of Steve and lead them in a discussion that addresses the following questions: What message should we send to kids? Could any of Steve's experiences been avoided? If you had been Steve's teacher, what would some of you're academic and social goals have been? What could you have done to support him in meeting those goals? Then, play the second clip for the students. Again, lead the students in discussion that focuses on these questions: In what ways could have school better prepared Steve? How does this story reinforce a "strengths-based" approach to goal setting? What things should have been included in Steve's transitional plan?

Additional Resources: none

Test Question:
Activity. Write a transition plan for Steve.

[*Answer:* Plans should include: statement of parent and student involvement, goal setting, delineation of goal and objectives, list of activities to support goals, method of assessment of progress toward goals, list of agencies and services necessary, and transition counseling (if deemed appropriate).]

CHAPTER 6: ATTENTION DEFICIT HYPERACTIVITY DISORDER

Weblink 6.1 Children and Adults with Attention Deficit Disorder (CHADD)

Annotation: CHADD is a national organization that represents children and adults with AD/HD. Their web site provides information on memberships, legislations, advocacy, research, fact sheets, and products available for purchase. The section of the site highlighted in this activity is a report on controversial treatments for people with AD/HD.

Learning Objective: Learn about the validity of alternative treatments for AD/HD.

Faculty Note: As future educators, your students should be aware of unorthodox treatments that parents or other educators may "suggest" for use with their students. The CHADD article provides background information on a variety of these controversial treatments. The activity will allow your students to see how convincing the information provided by doctors, advocates, or organizations can be. In conjunction with the discussion on the importance of promoting research-proven methods, you should discuss with your students the need to respect the beliefs and practices of families—some of who are committed to these treatments.

Activity: Have students go the CHADD web site and click on "Unproven Treatments." Have each student, or pair of students, select one of the controversial treatments. Then, have each student search the web or other resources for organizations that advocate for that treatment. Class discussion starters: Why are parents susceptible to these unsupported treatments? How convincing is the information provided? What can be done to inform parents of how to evaluate treatment considerations?

Additional Resources:
- Feingold: http://www.feingold.org/indexx.html
- Hooked on Phonics and Irlen Lens: http://www.greenwoodinstitute.org/resources/resphon.html
- Irlen Scotopic Sensitivity: The Link to Autism: http://trainland.tripod.com/annep.htm
- Article by Helen Irlen: http://www.latitudes.org/learn02.html
- Open Focus "Drugless Treatment for ADHD": http://www.openfocus.com/
- Braincare, Inc.: http://www.braincare.com/

Test Question:
Multiple Choice. Which of the following treatment options is NOT advocated for students with ADHD:
   a. Feingold diet
   b. Structured environment
   c. Psychostimulants
   d. Direct instruction
   e.
[*Answer:* A]

Weblink 6.3 Attention Deficit Disorder: Beyond the Myths

Annotation: This article presents common myths about AD/HD and then provides factual information that discounts the myth. Myths include: (1) ADD does not really exist, (2) Children with ADD are no different from their peers; all children have a hard time sitting still and paying attention, (3) Only a few people really have ADD, (4) All children with ADD are hyperactive and have learning disabilities, and (5) Medication can cure students with ADD.

Learning Objective: Distinguish between myths and facts related to ADD. Become aware of how people within your community view ADD.

Faculty Note: This activity will guide your students in sorting out facts from myths in regard to ADD. The article provides solid information on this often misunderstood disability. Students can refer to the opening section of the chapter (p. 205) to see if the information provided on the web site is the same as the information in the text. Additionally, students should be encouraged to use the text when creating their ADD survey.

Activity: Have students read the myths and facts and then create a survey in which they have facts mixed with myths. Go to several friends, parents, siblings, and teachers to see how they rate in terms of distinguishing fact from myth. In class, collect the counts and see if teachers were more informed than lay people.

Additional Resources: Text page 205.

Test Question:
Fact/Myth. A poor diet, such as high levels of sugar and/or food additives, can cause ADD.

[*Answer:* Myth]

Activity 6.3 Annual Report to Congress

Annotation: The annual report to Congress reports current prevalence and placement figures on students who receive services under IDEA.

Learning Objective: Note trends in the identification rates of students under the OHI category.

Faculty Note: Students should first be aware that ADHD is not a separate category of special education under IDEA, but is a recognized disability and students are primarily served under the "other health impaired" (OHI) label. This activity will allow students to see the numbers of students identified as OHI and explore trends in identification.

Activity: Have students create a chart of the numbers of student identified under the category "OHI" for the last 10 years. Then, using information from previous chapters on prevalence and specific information from this chapter on changes in IDEA regulations, have students come up with three things that may contribute to the recent increase in OHI numbers.

Additional Resources: none

Test Question(s):
True/False. According to the 1997 Amendments to IDEA, AD/HD is now its own disability category.

[*Answer:* False—students with ADHD still are eligible under the OHI category, but ADHD is now specifically list under OHI]

Short Answer. Describe three reasons for the recent increase in the number of students identified at OHI.

[*Answer:* Answers should include: increased awareness of AD/HD and therefore, classification under the OHI category, potential over identification of boys, more accurate reporting, social/cultural changes that have put more students at risk]

Video 6.2 Eric

Annotation: Dr. Goldsmith discusses his psychological evaluation of Eric.

Learning Objective: Become aware of the various perspective of participants in the multi-disciplinary team.

Faculty Note: It is important for students to understand the various perspectives of the people involved in the decision to identify and place students. Often future educators will look at situations only in terms of the particular career that they have chosen. This activity will demonstrate how different interest groups may view the same information differently and therefore, raise awareness in how they present information.

Activity: Divide students into groups. Give each group a piece of paper that has "background" information. Each group will view the video under a different pretence. Assign each group one of the following roles: parents, other psychologist, special education teacher whose class Eric will be place in due to this evaluation (and a subsequent IEP meeting), general education teacher who has had Eric for the last 6 months.

On the background information sheet orient each group with statements like "You are Eric's parents, you agreed to an evaluation by a psychologist, now you are about to hear his professional opinion. As you listen, how do you feel? What questions do you have?" or "You are the general education teacher who has had Eric for the last 6 months. You have been documenting Eric's behavior and working with the intervention/child-study team trying to support Eric's behavior in your class. You and the team have finally recommended a professional evaluation. You believe that Eric needs more intensive services than you can provide in your class. As you listen to the psychologist, how do you feel? What questions do you have?" or "You are the special education teacher. You think that many of Eric's 'problems' come from lack of structure and a behavioral program that meets Eric's specific needs. As you listen to the psychologist, how do you feel? What questions do you have?"

Additional Resources: none

Test Question:
Short Answer. In what ways can teachers present information that is sensitive to the various perspectives of the participants in the multi-disciplinary team?

[*Answer:* Responses will vary. Appropriate answers could include soliciting information for all participants in a neutral mode prior to the meeting, using non-emotive language, preparing parents for the meeting with a pre-meeting conference, etc.]

Weblink 6.10 Assessment

Annotation: Internet Special Education Resources provides information on assessment procedures for the identification of learning disabilities and attention deficit disorders.

Learning Objective: Delineate the steps for the identification of ADHD.

Faculty Note: This handout could be part of the "disability notebook" that students create over the course of the class. Ideally, the notebook will contain information on characteristics, identification, educational programs, and resources.

Activity: Have students create a handout for teachers on the steps to assessment for ADHD. Make sure the handout includes detailed descriptions for each step and references where teachers could get more information.

Additional Resources:
- Children and Adults with Attention Deficit Disorder: http://www.chadd.org/
- LD OnLine Assessment section: http://www.ldonline.org/ld_indepth/assessment/assessment.html

Test Question:
True/False. Once a qualified physician has made the diagnosis of ADHD, the child automatically qualifies for special education serves.

[*Answer:* False—the decision is still made by the team and includes other assessment documentation such as child's history, checklists completed by teachers, parents, etc., and classroom observation documentation]

Audio 6.2 Phineas Gage

Annotation: Dr. Hallahan tells the story of Phineas Gage, a railroad worker who was injured in a bizarre accident. The changes in Phineas' behavior can be linked to specific parts of his brain that were damaged in the accident.

Learning Objective: Understand the function of the frontal lobes and their relationship to ADHD.

Faculty Note: This activity corresponds to information in the text on pages 213-214. The memorable story of Phineas Gage serves as mnemonic device for remembering the relationship between the frontal lobes and executive functions.

Activity: Play the audio clip of Dr. Hallahan telling the story of Phineas Gage. As students listen, have them write down as many of Gage's "post accident" characteristics as possible. Then, have the class discuss the similarities between Gage's behaviors and the behaviors of students with ADHD.

Additional Resources: none

Test Question:
Multiple Choice. The frontal lobes are responsible for:
   a. Broca's Area
   b. Executive functions
   c. Language
   d. Hyperactivity

[*Answer:* B]

Video 6.3 and 6. 4 Eric

Annotation: Eric's psychologist and therapist discuss what they are working on to help Eric. Goals include self-esteem, compliance, and appropriate communication.

Learning Objective: Recognize how interpersonal, self-esteem, and compliance goals relate to academic performance.

Faculty Note: Some students may be resistant to the goal of "compliance." This activity allows students to explore the relationship between such norm-based goals to success within schools and the workplace. You can extend this discussion to include factors that relate to successful adult outcomes (p. 232 of the text).

Activity: Watch the video clips and write 3 goals that they are working on with Eric. Determine which goals are student-directed and which are school-directed. Then, lead your students in a discussion over the importance or place of "compliance" as a behavioral goal. Discussion starters could include: What role do compliant behaviors play in schools? Is compliance a necessary skill in order to be successful? In what ways can compliance be viewed as a negative goal? What are ways to teach and reinforce compliance?

Additional Resources:
   • Shapiro, E., DuPaul, G. J., & Bradley-Klug, K. L. (1998). Self-management as a strategy to improve the classroom behavior of adolescents with ADHD. Journal of Learning Disabilities, 31, 545-555.

Test Question:
Essay. Describe a contingency-based self-management program.

[*Answer:* Answers will vary. Key features include: students keep track of their own behaviors and rewards/consequences are delivered based upon performance]

Activity 6.26 Jeremy and Ann

Annotation: Jeremy and Ann, adults with ADHD, describe their frustrations of living with the disorder.

Learning Objective: Using case examples, create a coaching script for two adults with ADHD.

Faculty Note: This activity allows students to explore the role of a "coach," as described in the text on page 235. To extend the activity, you could have students write coaching scripts for someone they know who may be having difficulty with organization, focusing on a big project, or meeting some other goal.

Activity: Have students read the box on page 231 of the text. Then, in pairs, have the students create a coaching script (see p. 235) for both Ann and Jeremy.

Additional Resources: none

Test Question:
Multiple Choice. An "coach" for someone with ADHD is someone who:
- a. provides emotional support and practical advice
- b. track medication dosages and behavioral responses
- c. provides a self-management program for the client
- d. works on decreasing ADHD symptoms through diet and exercise

[*Answer:* A]

CHAPTER 7: EMOTIONAL OR BEHAVIORAL DISORDERS

Weblink 7.1 Mental Health Internet Resources

Annotation: This link takes you directly to the Mental Health Internet Resources' glossary of mental health terms' section on "emotional disturbance/behavioral disorder." Links on from this definition are connected to definitions for "conduct disorder" and "oppositional defiant disorder."

Learning Objective: Distinguish among different behavioral labels.

Faculty Note: This activity will help students understand the different types of emotional or behavioral disorders. After students have completed the table, you can discuss with the students how the identification of these characteristics can inform instructional and behavioral programming.

Activity: Have students complete the following table by filling in example characteristics under each heading.

Conduct disorders	Anxiety-withdrawal	Immaturity	Socialized aggression

Additional Resources: none

Test Question:
True/False. A conduct disorder is a persistent pattern of behavior that involves violation of the rights of others.

[*Answer:* True]

Activity 7.6 Differences in Definitions

Annotation: This activity prompts students to compare the federal definition (p. 250) and the National Mental Health and Special Education Coalition definition (p. 251) and then come up with their own definition.

Learning Objective: Compare and contrast the two definitions, highlighting the advantages and disadvantages to both.

Faculty Note: As discussed in previous chapters, definitions have a tremendous influence on who gets identified, what services persons receive under that identification, and how the general public perceives the disability. This activity will have students carefully examine the subtle, or not-so-subtle, differences in definitions and make inferences about how such changes would influence identification rates and services.

Activity: Have students compare and contrast the differences in definitions by completing the table:

Definition	Key Points	Differences	Advantages/Disadvantages
Federal definition			
National Mental Health and Special Education Coalition definition			

Additional Resources: none

Test Question:
True/False. In the Federal definition of emotional disturbed, educational performance is clearly defined.

[*Answer*: False]

Weblink 7.8 Youth Violence: Society's Problem (actual link on Weblink 7.9)

Annotation: Hill Walker discusses the characteristics of aggressive and antisocial youth, risk factors associated with such patterns of behavior, long-term outcomes, and preventative strategies designed to reduce risk factors.

Learning Objective: Understand the conditions that place children at greater risk for developing aggressive or antisocial behaviors and learn about preventative approaches.

Faculty Note: Preservice or novice teachers can be reluctant to identify kids as "a pain in the neck." But the behaviors that some students exhibit do make it challenging to work with them and include them in group activities. Walker discusses what some of these challenging behaviors are and links such maladaptive behaviors to factors in the environment that place children at risk for developing these behaviors. The last section of the article briefly mentions preventative strategies. This activity will have students expand upon these recommendations and discuss ways to implement similar programs/policies in their community.

Activity: Have students read Hill Walker's article "Youth Violence: Society's Problem" and then have them, in groups, come up with early intervention strategies to try to reduce or mediate some of the factors Walker lists. Students should use the web and other resources to compile their recommendations.

Additional Resources:
- The Pacific Center for Violence Prevention: http://www.pcvp.org/
- Committee for Children: http://www.cfchildren.org/
- Rock Solid Foundation: http://www.rocksolid.bc.ca/
- Virginia Youth Violence Project: http://curry.edschool.virginia.edu/curry/centers/youthvio/
- Warning Signs: http://helping.apa.org/warningsigns/
- APA Public Policy Office: http://www.apa.org/ppo/violence.html

Test Question:
Short Answer. What are the five factors identified by researchers relating to youth violence and delinquency.

[*Answer:* (1) the mother and/or the father has been arrested, (2) the child has been a client of child protection, (3) one or more family transitions have occurred (death, divorce, trauma, family upheaval), (4) the youth has received special education services, and (5) the child has a history of early and/or severe antisocial behavior.]

Weblink 7.6 National Institute of Mental Health: Autism

Annotation: The National Institute of Mental Health (NIMH) conducts and gathers research related to mental illness. Research areas include: basic neuroscience, and behavioral science, and genetics. Their web site provides brochures and information sheets, reports, press releases, fact sheets, and other educational materials related to a variety of mental health conditions. Students will be directed to their section on autism for this activity.

Learning Objective: Learn about the characteristics and treatment options for autism.

Faculty Note: Students will have the opportunity to read in more detail about the characteristics and treatments for autism (p. 270).

Activity: Have students go to the NIMH section on autism: (http://www.nimh.nih.gov/publicat/autismmenu.cfm). Have them read the article "Unraveling Autism." Then complete a facts sheet to add to their reference resources for the class. Each fact sheet should include information on characteristics, identification, prevalence, and treatments.

Additional Resources:
- See NIMH's reference list: http://www.nimh.nih.gov/publicat/autismmenu.cfm

Test Question:
True/False. Pharmacological interventions (medication) can improve the behavioral and cognitive functioning of individuals with autism.

[*Answer:* True]

Weblink 7.8 Violence Resources

Annotation: The National Alliance for the Mentally Ill (NAMI) provides information related to policies and issues for people with mental illness. This activity will explore NAMI's "policy" statement on the use of seclusion and restraint for people with behavioral disorders.

Learning Objective: Identify students' rights in the use of seclusion and restraint for behavioral modification.

Faculty Note: Students in your class may have observed or be aware of classrooms that use seclusion or restraint as a[part of a behavioral program. It is important for students to know the legal issues associate with these methods and explore some of the controversial issues that surround such practices.

Activity: Have students go to the NAMI site, click on "Policy," scroll down to the "Were We Stand" section, and select the position paper on seclusion and restraint. Students should read the position paper prior to coming to class. In class, divide the students into small groups and have them discuss their reactions to the article. Then, in a large group, discuss the issues brought up in the article.

Additional Resources:
- Child Welfare League of America: http://www.cwla.org/cwla/secres/seclusionrestraints.html
- Alliance for Children and Families: http://www.alliance1.org/facts-April142000.asp
- Advocacy Unlimited, Inc.: http://www.mindlink.org/civillib.html

Test Question:
Short answer. Define the following terms, as they were presented in the NAMI article on seclusion and restraint: control of the environment, coercion, and punishment.

[*Answer:* **control of the environment** = actions taken by facilities to curtail individual behavior to avoid having to use adequate staffing or clinical interventions; **coercion** = designed solely to force the patient to comply with the staff's wishes; or **punishment** = actions taken by staff to punish or penalize patients.]

Activity 7.15 Amy

Annotation: Amy's mother describes some of the characteristics that set Amy apart from typically developing children.

Learning Objective: Explore interventions for the behaviors of social withdrawal, suicidal tendencies, and hostility.

Faculty Note: Amy's past behaviors included both externalizing and internalizing behaviors (pp. 265-268). In this activity, students will research behavioral strategies designed to reduce or eliminated these maladaptive behaviors.

Activity: Have students view the video clip of Amy's mother discussing Amy's behaviors 2 years ago. Obviously, Amy has improved a great deal since then. For this project, have your students investigate strategies to deal with the behaviors of social withdrawal, suicidal tendencies, and hostility.

Behavior	Description	Strategy
Social Withdrawal		
Suicidal Tendencies		
Hostility		

Additional Resources:
- Suicide Prevention Advocacy Network: http://www.spanusa.org/
- San Francisco Suicide Prevention: http://www.sfsuicide.org/index2.html

- Suicide Prevention Communications Project: http://www.aifs.org.au/external/ysp/menu.html

Test Question:
Short Answer. List 3 early warning signs associated with suicide.

[*Answer:* Responses can include any of the following: recent loss, change in personality, change in behaviors, change in sleep patterns, change in eating habits, fear of losing control, diminished sexual interest, and low self-esteem.]

Audio 7.2 Preventing Prevention

Annotation: Dr. Kauffman discusses how systems fail to prevent the development of emotional or behavioral disorders. He alludes to an article he wrote in Exceptional Children on the prevention of prevention and challenges students to consider why schools fail to engage in such practices as school-wide discipline procedures and early intervention supports at the first sign of behavioral problems.

Learning Objective: Understand the various ways in which schools and society fail to address the early intervention of emotional or behavioral disorders.

Faculty Note: Students will read Kauffman's take on how society often acts in opposition to what it advocates in rhetoric. See if your students can come up with examples of their own the demonstrate this act of "preventing prevention."

Activity: Have students read Kauffman's 1999 article on preventing prevention. Then, have students select 3 of the examples listed and come up with specific policies or ways in which this activity can being carried out.

Additional Resources:
- Kauffman, J. M. (1999). How we prevent the prevention of emotional and behavioral disorders. Exceptional Children, 65(4), 448-468.

Test Question:
Essay. List and discuss 3 ways that Kauffman believes schools and society at large engage in the "prevention of prevention."

[*Answer:* Possible answers include: an overriding concern for labels, objecting to a medical model of services, preferring false negatives to false positives, calling special education ineffective, misconstruing the least restrictive and least intrusive intervention, complaining of the costs associated with special education, maintaining developmental optimism, denouncing disproportionate identification, defending diversity, and denying or dodging deviance.]

CHAPTER 8: COMMUNICATION DISORDERS

Audio 8.2 Problems for All of Us

Annotation: Dr. Kauffman discusses the variety of possible communication disorders including speaking, understanding, writing, and reading. He encourages students to considers factors the make such challenges worse.

Learning Objective: Understand the factors that contribute to exacerbating difficulties in communicating.

Faculty Note: This activity is a great one to set the tone for the chapter. In this activity, students will be able to draw parallels from communication difficulties they may have to the difficulties encountered by those with communication disorders.

Activity: First, ask the students to spend a few minutes thinking about which of the communication tasks listed by Dr. Kauffman is most intimidating or difficult for them and which factors serve to exacerbate their difficulty. Then, have the students get with a partner to share their answers. Have the students work with each other to share strategies for dealing with these issues. Bring the class back together and create a list of the strategies suggested.

Additional Resources: none

Test Question:
True/False. All communication disorders involve speech.

[*Answer:* False]

Activity 8.2 What is the Difference?

Annotation: Students are given examples of disorders and must determine whether they are speech disorders or language disorders. Immediate feedback on their responses is provided.

Learning Objective: Distinguish between speech and language goals.

Faculty Note: It is important for students to understand the difference between speech and language goals (p. 298). Many speech problems, with appropriate, early, and intensive intervention, can be reduced or eliminated. Yet, as students get older, speech goals may be dropped altogether or minimized as the effectiveness of intervention is decreased. This activity will reinforce the difference between speech and language goals.

Activity: Have students complete Activity 8.2 and check their responses. Then, have them select 1 speech disorder and 1 language disorder and write a behavioral objective for each.

Additional Resources:
- Table 8.2: Patterns of Development (p. 302)

Test Question:
Multiple Choice. Appropriate speech goals include all of the following EXCEPT:

    a. articulation
    b. fluency
    c. pragmatics
    d. producing voice

[*Answer:* C—pragmatics would be a language goal]

Weblink 8.1 American Speech-Language-Hearing Association

Annotation: ASHA is the professional credentialing association for audiologists, speech-language pathologists, and speech, language, and hearing scientists. Their web site provides information on advocacy, research, treatments, policy, job searches, pathology, and membership. The section covered in this activity is "IDEA 1997 Questions and Answers," a question and answer guide to changes in practice required by new IDEA regulations.

Learning Objective: Understand the how changes in IDEA will affect speech and language services.

Faculty Note: This activity is particularly helpful for students who are preparing to become special or general educators, but not speech/language pathologists. Therefore, they will not get specific training in the application of IDEA to SLP services. Understanding these connections will better prepare the future educators to support and co-develop appropriate SLP goals.

Activity: Direct students to the section on the ASHA web site regarding IDEA regulations and speech/language services (http://www.asha.org/idea/idea_q&a.htm). Students can get to this page by clicking on "Advocacy" on the home page, then selecting "Education," and finally, selecting "Individual's with Disabilities Education Act—special section." Direct students to the FAQ sheet. Have students read the frequently asked questions and answers. Students should then create a fact sheet that highlights questions they believe are important for teaching to know.

Additional Resources: none

Test Question:
Short Answer. Respond to the following question posed by ASHA: How will the need to "address general education/curriculum " affect the role of the SLP?

[*Answer:* "Framing benchmarks in curriculum language will ensure that both the special educator and the classroom teacher are addressing the objective, and that the effect of the child's disability on achievement is the focus of special education services." (from the ASHA web site)]

Weblink 8.4 Speech and Language Therapy in Practice

Annotation: Speech and Language Therapy is an independent, quarterly magazine that focuses upon sharing information that is practical and immediately applicable. The articles are intended to provoke thought about one's practice.

Learning Objective: Identify key areas of language development that can be integrated into general education instruction.

Faculty Note: Many of your students may have never observed an SLP or even seen speech and language goals. In this activity, students can read about what SLP's do and begin to get ideas on how to support speech and language goals in their classrooms.

Activity: Have students click on the "Articles" section of the home page. Then, have each student read the article "Should Teacher Have More Training in Language Development." After reading the article, each student should write a reflection/response paper (no more than 2 pages) in which they examine the issues discussed in the paper and the influence such training would have on their future teaching.

Additional Resources: none

Test Question:
Essay. Describe 3 ways in which teachers can promote language development in their classes.

[*Answer:* Responses can include: instruction in grammar, verb tense production, lengthening sentences, asking questions, and vocabulary development.]

Audio 8.3 Efficiency and Authenticity

Annotation: Dr. Kauffman discusses augmented or alternative means of communication and how these should be evaluated in terms of efficiency and authenticity. He challenges students to consider the question of "authenticity."

Learning Objective: Articulate the ethical and educational problems associated with the lack of "authenticity" of an alternative or augmented means of communication.

Faculty Note: This activity corresponds to information on augmentative and alternative communication on pages 317-322. Some students may be unfamiliar with augmentative communication devices. For this activity, it may be helpful to bring in some examples or to show a video that demonstrates communication alternatives.

Activity: Have students work in small groups to determine strategies for making decisions about the authenticity of an alternative communication device or approach. Each group should come up with a specific example of an alternative or augmentative means of communication and then prescribe a procedure for testing its authenticity. Groups should share their approaches with each other and discuss the ethical ramifications to problems with authenticity.

Additional Resources:
- Facilitative Communication Institute: http://soeweb.syr.edu/thefci/
- Resolution on Facilitative Communication by the American Psychological Association: http://web.syr.edu/~thefci/apafc.htm
- Vermont Facilitative Communication Network: http://www.uvm.edu/~uapvt/faccom.html
- Assistive Technology Industry Association: http://www.atia.org/
- Augmentative Communications Consultants, Inc.: http://www.acciinc.com/
- The Great Talking Box Company: http://www.djtech.com/GTB/gtb.htm

Test Question:
Essay. Define efficiency and authenticity in terms of augmentative and alternative means of communication. Then discuss why "authenticity" can carry ethical ramifications as well.

[*Answer:* Efficiency refers to the speed and the easy with which one can communicate; Authenticity refers to the fact that the message/communication comes from the person with the disability. Authenticity is important because it would be a violation of a persons rights to, in essence, "put words in their mouth."]

Weblink 8.13 The Multicultural Electronic Journal of Communication Disorders (MEJCD)

Annotation: MEJCD is an electronic journal (available only on the web) whose mission is to provide information on multicultural issues in the field of speech and language pathology.

Learning Objective: Learn about the relationship between cultural factors and communication patterns.

Faculty Note: All articles from the journal focus upon issues relating to the interaction of culture and communication. Many of them include helpful hints for teachers or guiding questions that teachers can use when evaluation instructional programs.

Activity: Have students select an article from either volume 1 or 2 of the journal and then write a summary of the statement. Students can then share their summaries with the class. Class discussion should be on the relevance of the issues to instructional practices.

Additional Resources: none

Test Question:
Essay. In what ways can models of service delivery that include the prescription of expensive technology, and frequent visits to several different members of a healthcare services delivery team, e.g., speech-language pathologists, physical and occupational therapists, rehabilitation engineers, computer access specialists, and so forth be counter to the culture of the family.

[*Answer:* Responses will vary, but could address issues of cultural mistrust, financial resources, views of health, disability, and/or technology, and family/community values.]

Weblink 8.20 American Academy of Audiology

Annotation: The American Academy of Audiology is the largest professional organization for audiologists. The AAA's mission is to provide professional development through education and research.

Learning Objective: Collect information about hearing aids.

Faculty Note: Hearing aids are often misunderstood. People may think that all persons with hearing loss can successfully use a hearing aid or that the sound provided by a hearing aid is just like that of someone with normal hearing. This FAQ page will answer these questions and dispel other myths your students may have in regard to hearing aids.

Activity: Have student go to the "Consumer Resources" and then open "Frequently Asked Questions about Hearing Aids." Student should read the FAQ and then come up with one "quiz" question. Student can bring their questions to class and you can read the questions and tally responses.

Additional Resources: none

Test Question:
True/False. The sounds produced by digital hearing aids sound remarkably similar to the hearing of people without hearing loss.

[*Answer:* False]

CHAPTER 9: HEARING IMPAIRMENT

Activity 9.2 Myth vs. Fact

Annotation: Students test their understanding of deafness by reading questions and responding "myth" or "fact."

Learning Objective: Research background information related to unknown facts about deafness.

Faculty Note: Students will be able to check their prior knowledge of deafness and ASL and then, independently research information related to questions they still may have. Provide students an opportunity to share what they have learned with others in the class, either through a newsgroup/online discussion or by group discussion in class.

Activity: Have students complete Activity 9.2 and then get their score. Students should select 2 questions (particularly ones they missed) and gather background information on those questions.

Additional Resources:
- American Sign Language Teachers' Association: http://www.aslta.org/
- Hear My Hands: http://www.hearmyhands.org/
- American Sign Language: http://www.signmedia.com/info/asl.htm
- Deaf Culture: http://www.deafmall.net/deaflinx/culture.html
- Deaf World Web: http://dww.deafworldweb.org/
- Deafness.about.com: http://deafness.about.com/health/deafness/

Test Question:
True/False. Deaf culture refers to the believe that deafness is not a "pathology" rather it way of living, communicating, and interacting with the world.

[*Answer:* True]

Weblink 9.2 National Association for the Deaf

Annotation: The National Association of the Deaf (NAD) private, non-profit organization representing accessibility and civil rights of the deaf and hard of hearing.

Learning Objective: Gain a greater understanding of the access and civil right issues for the deaf and hard of hearing.

Faculty Note: Some of your students will not be aware of the unique access and civil rights issues related to the deaf and hard of hearing. This activity will give them the opportunity to explore current political issues related to hearing disabilities. Although the text mentions one controversial topic, often referred to as the "oral-mannualism" debate (p. 359), this activity will demonstrate a variety of others issues—particularly of older people with hearing disabilities.

Activity: Have students go to the NAD site and locate a particular issue that NAD is advocating. The web site contains press releases, articles, and conference briefs that all contain NAD issues. Students should read the about the topic and write a brief summary statement. Allow the students an opportunity to share what they have learned with others.

Additional Resources: none

Test Question:
Short Answer. Name 2 ways ADA can protect the rights of someone who is deaf or hard of hearing.

[*Answer:* Appropriate answers can include: availability of an interpreter, access to TDD or captioning technology, protection against discriminatory practices, protection from exclusion in schools or from a job due to deafness, access to medical treatment—hospitals must have communication options for the deaf]

Weblink 9.3 Deaf World Web

Annotation: Deaf World Web is an extensive web site devoted to the issues and information pertinent to the deaf. The site includes a "Deaf Encyclopedia" that provides background information and resources on topics A-Z. Deaf World Web also provides country-specific information, including deaf population, schools and services, and sign language used.

Learning Objective: Use the Deaf World Web to gather information about a topic related to deafness.

Faculty Note: As the students read through the chapter, the information may create more questions than answers. This activity will allow students to explore in more detail some of the issues that are in the text (such as deaf culture, biomechanics of the ear, bilingual-bicultural, speech-reading, and technology) as well as allow students to explore issues that are not in the text.

Activity: Have students get into pairs and then assign each pair a different letter of the alphabet. Students should then go to the Deaf World Web site and select a topic under their letter. Students can read the background information and explore the provided related links. Finally, have students write a one-page summary/description of the topic. Summaries can be collected and kept in three-ring binder for others to share.

Additional Resources: none

Test Question:
True/False. The deaf population in the United States is approximately .5%.

[*Answer:* True]

Weblink 9.7 House Ear Institute

Annotation: The House Ear Institute is a non-profit research center that provides information related to treatments for hearing disabilities.

Learning Objective: Understand what cochlear implants are, considerations for surgery, and outcomes for people implants.

Faculty Note: This activity corresponds with "The Controversy Surrounding Cochlear Implants" on page 358 of the text.

Activity: Have students go on a mission to collect information on cochlear implants. See if they can find pro and con statements regarding this treatment. Students should reference where they got their information using a chart similar to the one below. Have students share their information with others by leading them in a discussion of cochlear implants.

Institute, Organization, or Other	Web Address	Information Provided

Additional Resources:
- University of Texas at Dallas Cochlear Implant Laboratory: http://www.utdallas.edu/~loizou/cimplants/
- Shea Center for Ears, Hearing, and Balance: http://www.ears.com/
- American Ear: http://www.americanear.com/
- Hearing Innovations Inc.: http://www.hearinginnovations.com/

Test Question:
Essay. Describe cochlear implants and summarize the key points in the debates that surround them.

[*Answer:* Responses should include surgical procedure for implant, overview of how the implants work, and then discussion related to whether or not deafness is a disability or a characteristic and questions related to effectiveness of the implant.]

Activity 9.20 Inclusion for Everyone?

Annotation: This activity has students explore position statements related to the inclusion of deaf students in general education settings. Probes stimulate students to define why issues of inclusion are framed differently by those in the deaf community from those of other disability-advocacy groups.

Learning Objective: Articulate the "anti-inclusion" position held by some members of the deaf community.

Faculty Note: In this activity students will read statements from parents, advocacy organizations, and people concerned about the rights of the deaf and hard of hearing. After reading these statements, students should have a better understanding of those who advocate for the preservation of a "deaf culture." This activity will also be a good introduction to other discussions related to issues of mannualism vs. oralism, cochlear implants, etc.

Activity: Have students go to the section on Deaf World Web on "inclusion." Students should read several of the articles. Lead students in a discussion that used the following discussion starter: "How would you respond to a parent of a deaf child who was seeking advice on educational options?"

Additional Resources: none

Test Question:
True/False. Some people within the deaf community believe that too much mainstreaming is a threat to the Deaf culture.

[*Answer:* True]

Weblink 9.26 Gallaudet University

Annotation: Gallaudet University is a four-year, liberal arts university for students who are deaf or hard of hearing.

Learning Objective: Compare and contrast the services, opportunities, and experiences students at Gallaudet University have with those at your institution.

Faculty Note: This activity will allow students to learn about university experiences for deaf and hard of hearing students at a university specifically designed to meet their unique needs. The activity corresponds to the information on transition on pages 373-375 of the text.

Activity: Have students explore the Gallaudet web site—looking at course options, departments, athletics, social events, etc. Then, have them explore these same areas on your university web site. Students can then complete a Venn diagram in which they compare and contrast their experiences and opportunities with those of students at Gallaudet.

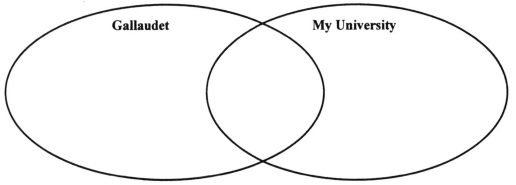

Additional Resources: Your university web site.

Test Question:
Essay. Describe how the experiences of a Gallaudet student would be similar to yours? How would it be different? In what ways does Gallaudet prepare students for post-university life that is similar to your institution? Different?

[*Answer:* Responses will vary]

CHAPTER 10: VISUAL IMPAIRMENT

Activity 10.1 Thinking it Over

Annotation: John discusses why he enjoys being blind.

Learning Objective: Assess background knowledge related to blindness.

Faculty Note: This activity is a great way to introduce the chapter on visual impairments. Having students think about what they know (or think they know) about the topic creates a schema for students to attach information presented in the chapter. At the end of chapter, pass the K and W sections back to the students and have them complete the L section.

Activity: Have students watch the video of John discussing the advantages of his blindness. Then have students complete the K and W sections of a K-W-L chart on blindness and visual impairments.

Know-What do you know about visual impairments?	Want to Know—What information would you like?	Learned—After spending time learning about visual impairments, what have you learned?

Additional Resources: none

Test Question:
True/False. Braille is of no value for those with low vision.

[*Answer:* False]

Weblink 10.2 American Foundation of the Blind

Annotation: The American Foundation of the Blind's web site provides information on support for the blind, conference information, press releases, and links to other web resources. The section explored in this activity deals with ways to provide assistance for people who are blind.

Learning Objective: Learn about how the electronic book publishing market serves people who are blind or with low vision.

Faculty Note: In the article, the author's state "access to information is profoundly critical in determining a person's quality of life." Some of your students may take for granted all of the information that is easily accessible to them through print. This activity will stimulate them to think about what they have read recently and then see if it is available in a format that is accessible to someone with a visual impairment.

Activity: Have students go to the American Federation of the Blind site and then scroll down to "Surpassing Gutenberg" an article on electronic books and the future of access to reading materials for the blind now and even more so in the near future. Students should read the article and then do a search for how many books they have read recently that are available in electronic form (or in another form accessible to people who are blind or with low vision). Students can fill out a form (similar to the one below) to keep track of the books.

Title of Book	Forms Available (i.e., electronic, Braille, or large print0	Where to Purchase?

Additional Resources:
Sources of electronic books:
- E-book Mall: http://www.ebookmall-ebooks.com/
- Alexandria Digital Literature: http://www.alexlit.com/start.taf?hallpass=lJvuDixU
- E-books for You: http://www.ebooksforyou.com/
- The Electronic Bookseller: http://www.electronicbookseller.com/

Test Question:
<u>Short Answer.</u> Describe the "Digital Talking Book" and how it can transform the reading experience for people who are blind or with low vision.

[*Answer:* Digital Talking Books can provide full text that can be automatically displayed in Braille or in large print fonts. Books are also "read" by narrative and can be listened to.]

Activity 10.6 How Does Prevalence Affect Parents?

Annotation: This activity asks students to respond to three questions related to issues of low prevalence—with such small numbers how are these students best served?

Learning Objective: Explore service delivery models for students with vision disabilities.

Faculty Note: This activity corresponds to the discussion of service delivery models on pages 412-413 of the text.

Activity: Prior to class, have students read and respond to the questions provided in Activity 10.6. In class, divide the students into 4 groups--"parents," "administrators," "special educators," and "general educators." Each group should come up with pro's and con's to the use of itinerant teachers for the delivery of services for students with visual impairments.

Additional Resources: none

Test Question:
Short Answer. Define "itinerant teacher" and explain why this term is usually associated with the provision of services for students with visual impairments.

[*Answer:* An itinerant teacher is a special educator who works with students (and their teachers) in several different schools. Due to the low numbers of students with visual impairments, itinerant teachers are usually the most cost effective way to provide services to a number of students across a district or region.]

Weblink 10.5 National Eye Institute

Annotation: The National Eye Institute provides information for researchers, educators, healthcare professionals, and the media. The section explored in this activity is a collection of pictures that depict various eye diseases.

Learning Objective: Understand how various impairments result in different kinds of visual difficulties.

Faculty Note: The material in this activity corresponds to the "Causes" section in the textbook (pp. 390-393). In this activity students will be able to link descriptive information from the text to visual depictions of the diseases.

Activity: Have students look at the different visual impairments and learn about the different visual difficulties someone could have. Students should complete a chart that will help them to differentiate among the different disabling conditions.

Condition	Definition/Etiology of the Condition	Describe (in your own words) what the picture looked like

Additional Resources: none

Test Question:
Short Answer. What is diabetic retinopathy and in what ways does it affect vision.

[*Answer:* Diabetic retinopathy is a condition resulting from lack of blood supplied to the retina. (It is also the fastest-growing cause of blindness). Vision would look like someone had blacked out parts of a scene.]

Weblink 10.12 How Do You?

Annotation: This article is set-up in a question and answer format with the questions provided by children who are interested in finding out about how people who are blind function.

Learning Objective: Learn

Faculty Note: Students who have never known or interacted with someone who is blind may have questions similar to those asked by children. This site allows students to read the questions and answers without having to ask them themselves!

Activity: Students should read the questions and answers. Then, lead students in a discussion about how these issues can be addressed within the classroom. You can create a chart on the board (or overhead) to take notes of the students' ideas.

Question	Response	Classroom Application

Additional Resources: none

Test Question:
Essay. In the "Questions From Kids About Blindness" article, many questions are posed and answered. Describe two things you learned about from reading this article.

[*Answer:* Answers will vary but can include: How do blind people...identify food, clothes, money; play card games; use a cane; cook; tell time; go to school; and cross the street.]

Weblink 10.15 Library Services for the Blind and Physically Handicapped

Annotation: The National Library Service for the Blind and Physically Handicapped (NLS) is a division of the Library of Congress. NLS provides a free library program of Braille and recorded materials to borrowers by postage-free mail through a network of cooperating libraries.

Learning Objective: Learn about the services that NSL provides and how to get access to those services.

Faculty Note: Knowing about this valuable resources will be important for your future educators who may serve (or be in contact with those who serve) students who are blind or have low vision.

Activity: Have students explore the "Library" site and search for answers to the following questions: Who is eligible? How do you sign-up? What services are available? What does a talking book sound like? What is Web-BLIND?

Additional Resources: none

Test Question:
Essay. How does the law help people with visual disabilities get access to alternative print materials?

[*Answer:* Students are protected under IDEA, which means at no cost to the individual (or family) accessible materials should be provided. ADA allows for reasonable accommodations in the workplace, which may include note takers, readers, Braille, audio recordings, and large-print materials.]

Weblink 10.20 Action for the Blind

Annotation: Action for the Blind is a charity that advocates for civil rights related to work, leisure activities, housing, and support for the blind.

Learning Objective: Identify concerns related to independent living of people who are blind.

Faculty Note: As students are considering what appropriate transition services for people with visual impairments should include (pp. 414-418), this activity will give them insight into some of the skills that are requisite for independent living.

Activity: Have students explore the Action for the Blind site. One couple on the site state: "It's so important to have a safe and secure environment where we can still retain our independence." As you look at the housing considerations, make a list of accommodations that would be necessary for independent living. Additionally, list the types of skills someone would need to live independently.

Additional Resources: none

Test Question:
True/False. Most people who are blind would rather have access to jobs and independent living than medical treatment and counseling.

[*Answer:* True]

CHAPTER 11: PHYSICAL DISABILITIES

Audio 11.1 Prevention: Where to? Where from?

Annotation: Dr. Kauffman discusses issues related to the prevention of physical disabilities.

Learning Objective: Examine the complex relationship between individual rights and the need for the protection of individuals.

Faculty Note: When a tragedy occurs and results in a physical disability, those involved with the situation can become concerned about preventing such occurrences in other people's lives. This may result in a laws being passed that are intended to reduce or eliminate future accidents. Yet, some people are resistant to such laws (seat belts are a good example) and feel like they should be able to make decisions for themselves. Audio clip 11.1 can be used as a good discussion starter to stimulate discussion related to these issues.

Activity: Brainstorm with your class ways in which society can "boost" preventative measures—especially those that would decrease the occurrence of traumatic brain injury. Then, explore the how some of those measures may infringe upon individual's rights.

Additional Resources: none

Test Question:
Essay. In the debate between individual rights and protection of individuals, where do you stand and why?

[*Answer:* Response will vary according to individual beliefs.]

Weblink 11.3 Disability Statistics Center

Annotation: The Disability Statistics Center provides statistical reports on information related to disabilities.

Learning Objective: Explore the incidence rates, causes, and educational considerations of TBI.

Faculty Note: This activity corresponds to information on traumatic brain injury in the text on pages 429-431. Student may be shocked by some of the information provided—especially, how preventable many of the causes are or that child abuse is one causal agent. You should help students focus upon the preventative recommendation in the article and have them think of ways classroom teachers can promote safety awareness.

Activity: Have students go to the Disability Statistics Center and search for "traumatic brain injury." Students should read the article and then respond to the following questions: What statistics surprised you the most? What thoughts did you have while reading the article? What actions might you engage in as a result of reading the article? If you could share one piece of information with parents, what would it be? What about teachers?

Additional Resources: none

Test Question:
True/False. The highest rate of TBI is among males, ages 25-35.

[*Answer:* False—male, youths]

Weblink 11.6 United Cerebral Palsy Association

Annotation: United Cerebral Palsy is an international organization that advocates for the rights of individuals with disabilities. Their web site includes information on education, employment, housing, parenting, sports and leisure, and travel.

Learning Objective: Define cerebral palsy. Be able to discuss prevention and treatment options related to CP.

Faculty Note: This activity corresponds with the information in the text on pages 431-433. After students have created a fact sheet, encourage them to explore other sections of the web site.

Activity: Have students go to the UCP web site and enter the "Parents and Families" section. Students should read the section "Cerebral Palsy - Facts & Figures." Then complete a fact sheet.

Question	Information
What is cerebral palsy?	
What are the effects?	
What are the causes? What are they types?	
Can it be prevented?	
Can cerebral palsy be treated?	
Is research being done on cerebral palsy?	

Additional Resources: none

Test Question:
True/False. "Congenital" cerebral palsy means that the condition is related to the development and childbearing processes.

[*Answer:* True]

Weblink 11.8 Spina Bifida Association

Annotation: The Spina Bifida Association is a non-profit association that provides information on education, treatment, and prevention of Spina Bifida. In this activity students are directed to the "Education" section of their web site that provides informational articles on a variety of prevention and treatment topics.

Learning Objective: Learn about a latex allergy common to people with Spina Bifida.

Faculty Note: The text provides background information on the educational implications for those with Spina Bifida (p. 436). The information students will get in this activity is in addition to text information. Encourage students to read other articles, such as the one on folic acid, that contain other specific information related to prevention and treatment.

Activity: Have students go to the Spina Bifida Association home page and click on "Educational Updates." Direct students to read the article on latex allergies. Then, in class, lead students in a discussion of how classroom teachers can manage such a serious allergy. See if students can come up with a list of safety precautions.

Additional Resources: none

Test Question:
True/False. The relationship between Spina Bifida and latex allergies is clearly understood.

[*Answer:* False]

Weblink 11.13 National Organization for Fetal Alcohol Syndrome

Annotation: NOFAS is a nonprofit organization dedicated to the prevention of fetal alcohol syndrome caused by alcohol consumption during pregnancy.

Learning Objective: Understand the causes and characteristics of FAS.

Faculty Note: This activity corresponds with the "Other Conditions Affecting Health or Physical Ability" section of the text (pp. 438-439). The discussion on FAS should be linked to prevention discussions as well as discussion of the educational implications.

Activity: Have students go to the NOFAS web site and have students collect examples of preventative campaigns spearheaded by NOFAS. Lead your students in a discussion related to how teachers could make use of the information provided on the site.

Additional Resources: none

Test Question.
Short Answer. Describe the characteristics of children with Fetal Alcohol Syndrome and some educational considerations.

[*Answer:* Fetal Alcohol Syndrome is an umbrella term that encompasses mental and physical birth defects that can include mental retardation, growth deficiencies, central nervous system dysfunction, craniofacial abnormalities and behavioral maladjustment's. Educational interventions can include: instruction in organizational strategies, use of task analysis when planning for instruction, creating a structured and consistent learning environment, and providing opportunities to strengthen self-determination.]

Activity 11.21 Teenage Pregnancies

Annotation: Students are prompted to make recommendations on programs that would reduce the number of teenage pregnancies.

Learning Objective: Evaluate several programs designed to prevent teen pregnancies or programs that support teen mothers, therefore reducing the number of babies being born with disabilities.

Faculty Note: Students may wonder why a section on teenage pregnancies is included in a text on special education. It is important to point out the relationship between teen pregnancies and the probability of giving birth to premature or low birth weight babies—two conditions that correlate later with difficulties in school. This relationship is defined in the text on pages 439-440.

Activity: Have student read the section "Prevention of Physical Disabilities" in the text on page 439. Then, have students do a web search for teen pregnancy prevention and support programs.

Additional Resources:
- Profile of teenage pregnancies: http://www.upm.edu.ph/bagumbayan/jan1999/1teenage.html
- Hagenhoff, C., Lowe, A., Hovell, M. F., Rugg, D. (1987). Prevention of the teenage pregnancy epidemic: A social learning theory approach. Education and Treatment of Children, 10, 67-83.
- Teenage Pregnancies: http://www.catholicdoctors.org.uk/CMQ/Indiv%20Articles/teen_preg_aug_1999.htm
- Bittersweet Findings Concerning Teenage Pregnancies: http://www.teenvoice.com/realtime/newarticles/pregnancies/

Test Question:
Essay. Describe the relationship between teenage pregnancies and children with disabilities. What are some ways to prevent teen mothers giving birth to kids with disabilities.

[*Answer:* Teen mothers are at a greater risk of giving birth to premature or low-birth weight babies due to inadequate prenatal care, having infections during pregnancy, poor nutrition, and anemia. Prevention can include access to better health care, better nutrition, and avoidance of pregnancy.]

Weblink 11.1

Annotation: WeMedia is a multi-media company designed for individuals with disabilities, their family and friends. WeMagazine is their lifestyle magazine devoted to the same mission.

Learning Objective: Explore an online magazine devoted to issues and information related to people with disabilities.

Faculty Note: WeMagazine covers everything from sports and leisure to politics and finances. By reading the online articles, students may get a slightly different perspective on current issues, such as the Presidential Campaign or recent ADA legislation.

Activity: Have students explore the magazine and then write a review it. Students should compare the topics and information to other lifestyle magazines.

Additional Resources: Other lifestyle magazines.

Test Question:
True/False. People with disabilities are excluded from mainstream sporting competitions, such as the Olympics or professional golf, but can participate in a variety of alternative competitions.

[*Answer:* False]

CHAPTER 12: SPECIAL GIFTS AND TALENTS

Activity 12.1 Thinking it Over

Annotation: Students will read brief case notes that describe the behaviors and interests of two young people. Given that information, they must decide if the student would qualify for gifted and talented.

Learning Objective: Understand the diversity of characteristics of people who are gifted and talented.

Faculty Note: This activity is a good introduction to the chapter on gifts and talents. For some students understanding why a person with a physical disability or mental disability needs special considerations is obvious, yet some people have difficulty understanding how having hyper-abilities can create the need for individualized instruction. Also, students may have preconceived notions about the characteristics of students who are gifted and talented and this activity works to dispel those as well.

Activity: Have students read the case descriptions and then decide whether or not the individual would qualify for services under the gifted and talented label. Divide students into groups and have them write down a list of "gifted" characteristics. Then, see if there is consensus among the groups as to what the characteristics are. Lead students in a discussion of the different definitions of giftedness and see if some the characteristics identified by the groups meet the various definitions.

Additional Resources: none

Test Question:
True/False. A person with special gifts do everything well.

[*Answer:* False]

Weblink 12.1 The Center for Talent Development

Annotation: The Center for Talent Development conducts academic talent searches, summer enrichment programs, seminars for parents, and leadership development workshops.

Learning Objective: Understand the relationship between giftedness and learning disabilities.

Faculty Note: This activity will help students understand comorbidity issues related to gifted/LD. Of particular concern is the problem with compensatory skills that the students may have the "mask" the learning disability, therefore, prolonging or preventing identification.

Activity: Have students go to "Resources" then to the "Online Articles" section of the CTD web site. Read the article "Underachievement and Learning Disabilities in Children Who Are Gifted" by Steven G. Zecker. Then have students write a one-page response to the question: What is the relationship between giftedness and learning disabilities.

Additional Resources:
- LD OnLine: http://www.ldonline.org

Test Question:
<u>Short Answer.</u> What are the difficulties with the identification of learning disabilities or ADHD comorbidity with giftedness?

[*Answer:* Student who are gifted and also have learning disabilities or ADHD, are often not identified as accurately or as early in their lives as their non-gifted peers. Early diagnosis and intervention are important for helping these students get access to services that would help reduce some of their learning difficulties.]

Weblink 12.4 National Association for Gifted Children

Annotation: NAGC is a non-profit organization that represents children with gifts and talents. The organization supports research and development as well as staff development in the area of gifted and talented.

Learning Objective: Identify what kinds of products are available for parents and teachers of gifted students.

Faculty Note: This activity will show students a sample of some of the information that is available for parents and teachers. After students spend some time looking at the materials, engage them in a discussion of ways to evaluate publications that are not peer reviewed. What are some ways teachers can determine the quality of suggestions and information provided? After the discussion, you can send your students to other web sites that sell materials and they can compare and contrast the different sites. This activity corresponds to information in the text, "Educational Considerations," pages 492-496.

Activity: Have your students go to the NAGC store and evaluate what kinds of materials are being sold. Students can evaluate the materials using the following guiding questions: Who is the target market for this videos and monographs? What would you assume about the research that is being presented—similar or different from information you would get in a scholarly journal?

Additional Resources:
- Gifted Education Press: http://www.cais.com/gep/
- Gifted Resources: Vendors: http://www.eskimo.com/~user/zvendors.html
- Hoagie's Gifted Resource Page: http://www.hoagiesgifted.org/gift.htm

Test Question:
<u>True/False.</u> Unlike students with disabilities, gifted students do not have a continuum of placement options—once identified gifted students receive services through separate classes.

[*Answer:* False]

Weblink 12.8 Buros Institute

Annotation: The Buros Institute provides information on commercially published tests. Their web site provides publisher information about a variety of tests as well as reviews of the tests.

Learning Objective: Identify the different intelligence tests that are commercially available.

Faculty Note: The text discusses the various definitions of giftedness and changes in the definition of giftedness (pp. 471-475). This activity will allow students to see descriptions for a variety of intelligence tests that seek to measure some of the different types of intelligence suggested in reform definitions.

Activity: Have students go to the Buros' web site and conduct a test locator search for "intelligence tests." Then, have student group the test into either "tradition intelligence test" or "alternative intelligence test" categories. After students have reviewed the tests, discuss as a class the advantages and disadvantages to looking beyond intelligence for giftedness.

Additional Resources: You may want students to view the tests or seek out additional information on a particular test. One source of information is:

- The Thirteenth Mental Measurements Yearbook. Edited by James C. Impara and Barbara S. Plake, 1998. [39-3422, ISBN 0-910674-54-X]

Test Question:
Short Answer. Name three different intelligence tests.

[*Answer:* Answers can include Slosson Intelligence Test, Kaufman Adolescent and Adult Intelligence Test, Social Intelligence Test: George Washington University Series, Culture Fair Intelligence Test, or Non-Verbal Intelligence Tests for Deaf and Hearing Subjects]

Weblink 12.14 Relations of Grouping Practices

Annotation: Students will read an online article discussing of the pro's and con's of homogeneous grouping practices for gifted (and non-gifted) students. The information comes from the American Association for Gifted Children web site.

Learning Objective: Identify pro's and con's of different instructional grouping practices for the gifted and talented.

Faculty Note: Students should refer to Table 12.2 on page 486 of their text for a summary of the possible effects of current educational reforms on the education of students who are gifted and talented.

Activity: Have students read the article "The Relationship of Grouping Practices to the Education of the Gifted and Talented Learner: Research-Based Decision Making" by Karen B. Rogers. Then divide students into groups of 4-5, have some groups take the position "Heterogeneous Grouping Benefits ALL Students" and the other groups take the position "Homogenous Grouping is the Most Efficient and Effective Way to Give ALL Students What They Need." See if your students can come to any definitive answers in regard to these complex issues. In what ways did the article support or refute their positions? Do the student think that there might be other research that would support an alternative point of view?

Additional Resources: none

Test Question:
Essay. Do you believe that the issues related to grouping practices (i.e., heterogeneous vs. homogenous ability grouping) differ for students with disabilities than the issues for students with hyperabilities? Why or why not?

[Answer: Answers will vary depending on student perspective]

Audio 12.2 Acceleration-When To Use It?

Annotation: Dr. Kauffman provides a case example of a child who has hyperabilities and then asks students to describe what an appropriate education for this child would look like—and could that education be provided without acceleration.

Learning Objective: Examine the issues related to acceleration.

Faculty Note: This activity corresponds with information in the text on page 496.

Activity: Play the audiotape (or have students listen to it on their own). Have them state what the issues are related to Aaron's education. Then, have students write about what kinds of educational experiences would be commensurate to his skills and provide challenge, too.

Aaron's Skills and Academic Needs	Educational Considerations

Additional Resources: none

Test Question:
Short Answer. What is the difference between acceleration and enrichment?

[*Answer:* Acceleration involves moving a child into a grade or placement ahead of his or her age peers. Enrichment means that students are engaged in projects or activities that specifically designed to challenge and stimulate talented students.]

Activity 12.27 Issues in Acceleration and Enrichment

Annotation: Students will read the case of Noshua Watson, a gifted and talented student who participated in the Program for the Exceptionally Gifted.

Learning Objective: Understand the issues associated with the acceleration of gifted students.

Faculty Note: Students may read the case of Noshua and generalize her positive experience to all gifted students. Yet, in order for students to be successful in such accelerated programs they need to have certain work and social skills. The discussion around this issue should highlight this fact.

Activity: Have students read the case study of an accelerated program on pages 494-495 of the text. Then, discuss why this program was particularly successful for Noshua. Possible discussion starters include: "What unique characteristics of Noshua made this program a good match?" "Can you think of some reasons why not all gifted students would thrive in this environment?" "Intelligence—or high SAT scores—was not the only factor the that the PEG program considered, why?"

Additional Resources: none

Test Question:
Essay. If you were to design an accelerated program, what kinds of characteristics would you look for in potential candidates?

[*Answer:* In order for students to be successful in accelerated programs they must possess emotional stability and maturity (as they will be with students who are older—sometime 4 years), they must have a strong work ethic (even though a student may be very bright, if they do not apply themselves, the program will not be successful), and they should posses specific talents in the area of specialization or interest.]

CHAPTER 13: PARENTS AND FAMILIES

Video 13.1 Mom

Annotation: Aviva, a parent of a student with disabilities, talks about what she believes should be parents' roles in the education of their children with special needs.

Learning Objective: Understand the important relationship that exists between parents and special education.

Faculty Note: Parents of students in special education have historically played a large role in the education of their children. Aviva touches upon many issues in her talk—ranging from the invested interest she has to the unique information she could provided that a teacher of many students might not have the time or capacity to know or understand. This activity will have students begin thinking about how parents should be involved and how to plan for that involvement.

Activity: Have students watch the video of Aviva talking about her role in the education of her daughter Lindsey. Aviva believes that it is the parents' responsibility to make sure that their children get the educational support that they need. In small groups, have students discuss the roles that they believe parents should play in their children's education. Guiding questions include: What unique information are parents in better position than teachers to provide? In what ways would you want parents to participate in the educational programming for their child? In what ways can parents be "too involved"—or can they?

Additional Resources: none

Test Question:
Essay. In what ways can teachers plan for the involvement of parents. Include specific examples.

[*Answer:* Responses will vary according to students perspective.]

Activity 13.3 Tomorrow's Children

Annotation: This NPR program explores the history of the treatment of children with disabilities. Audio excerpts of the original program, a copy of the transcript, and supporting materials are available on the site.

Learning Objective: Understand the historical views of disability and the sometime unique roles parents played.

Faculty Note: This NPR program is a powerful way for students to understand and explore the history of the treatment of disabilities. The stories told in the program provide a striking contrast to the services and rights now afforded to those with disabilities. It is interesting to explore with your students, however, how "remnants" of these views are still alive and well today.

Activity: Have students listen to the audio excerpt that describes Dr. Haiselden, a doctor in the early 1900's who publicly advocated for withholding treatment for children with disabilities, therefore allowing them to die.

Additional Resources: none

Test Question:
Essay. Why were terms like defective, idiot, and imbecile replaced with the word disability or more generally with "people first" language.

[*Answer:* Historical terms of defect, idiot, and imbecile are more value laden than current terms. Additionally, the terms "dehumanized" the individual—often he or she was replaced with the pronoun "it"—and therefore, excusing people from any moral obligation to the rights of that person.]

Activity 13.6 Stresses from the Public

Annotation: Bernadette Weih describes an unfortunate encounter with "well-intentioned" stranger while eating with her daughter who has severe disabilities and her son.

Learning Objective: Understand how public misconceptions about disabilities can add to the stress of having a child with a disability.

Faculty Note: Examples like this one make a strong point about how people, through their generalizations and assumptions, can insult people with disabilities (or their families). In this case, the ignorance is obvious, but many cases the comments are more subtle, but just a painful, harmful, or annoying. Encourage students to be aware of these "mis-ideas" and do their part to be better informed.

Activity: Have students read the story "Here's the Beef" and then see if they can think of examples of things that people say about or to people with disabilities that are misinformed or inappropriate. In this discussion, ask students why people "feel compelled" to walk across restaurants to make such statements and perhaps, what these statements reveal about the person making them. Finally, ask students how they would have liked to have responded and why do they think the mother responded in the way that she did.

Additional Resources: none

Test Question:
Short Answer. What things should one take into consideration when responding to an uniformed, layperson who has made an inappropriate statement about a person with a disability or disabilities in general?

[*Answer:* Answers can include: the relationship you have with this person, the background of the person, how responsive you believe they might be to "correct" information, how much time you want to spend educating this person, etc.]

Audio 13.2 What is Normal

Annotation: Dr. Hallahan challenges the notion of "dysfunctional" and "normal."

Learning Objective: Understand how assumptions about dysfunction can limit educators understanding of families and diminish the ways in which they are involved in the support of their children.

Faculty Note: This activity corresponds to the discussion of family systems theory on page 526.

Activity: Have students listen to Dr. Hallahan's discussion of dysfunction and normalcy. Then, have each student write a response paper in which they apply "Family Systems Theory" to an understanding of the relationship between families and schools.

Additional Resources:
- Just This Side of Normal: Glimpses into Life with Autism. Elizabeth King Gerlach. Four Leaf Press: June 1999.

Test Question:
Short Answer. Define "family systems theory."

[*Answer:* Family systems theory states that events that affect one member of the family also affect the other members, thus there is a reciprocal relationship among family members. Treatment and education should involve all members of the family.]

Video 13.7 Exceptional Parent

Annotation: Exceptional Parent's online magazine provides information, support, and ideas for parents and families of children with disabilities.

Learning Objective: Create a resources and information guide for parents.

Faculty Note: As your future educators think about planning for curriculum for their future students, they should also think about ways they can support the parents of their students. This activity allows students to explore the kinds of information they think would be good resources for parents.

Activity: Have students explore the Exceptional Parent web site. Then, in groups, have each group create a list of the kinds of information and resources they think would be good for teachers to make available for parents. Alternatively, students can design a newsletter for parents that highlight some of the information they found on the Exceptional Parent site.

Additional Resources: none

Test Question:
True/False. Professionals are always in the best position to help families of people with disabilities.

[*Answer:* False]

Test Bank: Interactive Companion

CHAPTER 1: EXCEPTIONALITY AND SPECIAL EDUCATION

1.1

Essay: List and describe four things that make special education different from general education.

[*Answer*: Appropriate responses include: individualized instruction, adherence to federal guidelines, continuum of alternative placements, FAPE requirement, instruction that is systematic, structured, and explicit, specialized training, and assessment requirements (typically more frequently than general education and progress monitoring more specified).]

1.2

Essay. Describe the steps necessary for identifying a student for special education.

[*Answer*: Students should include information related to parent notification, testing procedures, decision–making procedures, and procedural safeguards.]

1.3

Multiple Choice. Identify the correct order of the IEP process:
- a. evaluation, eligibility determination, IEP, services, IEP review, IEP re-eval
- b. evaluation, eligibility determination, IEP, services, IEP re-eval, IEP review
- c. eligibility determination, IEP, evaluation, services, IEP review, IEP re-eval
- d. IEP, evaluation, eligibility determination, IEP re-eval, IEP review

[*Answer*: B]

1.4

Essay. In what ways should making the distinction between "disability" and "handicap" influence teachers' instructional decisions.

[*Answer*: Teachers who understand this distinction are able to recognize things within the environment (such as physical, attitudinal, or instructional barriers) that serve as "handicaps" to the individual. Focusing upon what is in their control to change, they can work to reduce these handicaps and teach students ways to be successful despite their disability.]

1.5

Fill in the Blank.

1. _____ is the inability to do something or a diminished capacity to perform in a specific way.

2. _____ is a disadvantage imposed on an individual.

[*Answer*: (1) disability; (2) handicap]

1.6

Essay. Describe overall trends in the identification of students with disabilities. Include key factors related to the identification of certain disabilities and how that relates to identification patterns.

[*Answer:* Appropriate answers should include such things as the noted stability across disability categories that are easily identifiable such as physical disabilities or autism, increase in students identified as behavioral disordered and learning disabled as they get older, relatively low numbers of students identified as behavioral disordered compared to learning disabilities or speech/language impairments, higher numbers than expected of students identified at OHI—link to increased identification rates of ADHD, drop off of "developmentally delayed" label in some states after age 9, etc.]

1.7

True/False. The requirement for "reasonable accommodations" in ADA is similar to the FAPE requirement of IDEA in that both address the need for specially designed instruction.

[*Answer:* True]

1.8

Essay. You are a special education teacher who is about team-teach in a general education classroom next year. Write a letter to the general education teacher that delineates what you believe are your roles and responsibilities within his or her classroom. *hint: be as specific as possible

[*Answer:* Various responses. Appropriate responses will include the role of the IEP in instructional decision making, need for instruction that meets the needs of the student, need for clear expectations, active role within the instruction and management within the classroom, etc.]

1.9

Essay. In what ways to changes in language reflect changes in opportunities for children with disabilities?

[*Answer:* Various answers. Appropriate answers include reference to increased opportunities, higher expectations, and an emphasis on individual responsibility and power that have come with changing attitudes regarding disabilities.]

1.10

Essay. Dr. Kauffman suggests that the "appropriate education" aspect supersedes the "LRE" clause. What does that mean in terms of placement decisions? How should this be reflected in determining placement? Give specific examples for each.

[*Answer:* Various responses. Appropriate responses include the fact that IEP teams should first determine what the instructional goals and objectives are for an individual and then, they must determine how those goals can be met. Finally, teams should decide what the most supportive environment (with deference to LRE) for addressing those objectives is. Examples should be provided.]

CHAPTER 2: CURRENT TRENDS AND ISSUES

2.1

Essay. Dr. Christopher Kliewer makes the statement: "Inclusive education is nothing more than good teaching for all students." Given what you know about history of special education and the legal requirement for "specially designed instruction that meets the unusual needs of an exceptional student," in what ways can this statement be interpreted as true and in what ways can it be interpreted as false.

[*Answer*: Various responses. Appropriate answers should include specific examples of how good teaching equals effective teaching and therefore, the majority of students will benefit from what researchers support as effective teaching. Examples include clearly stating objectives, high levels of student engagement, repetition of concepts to mastery, and relevant and interesting content. On the other hand, what is needed for some students is not necessary for others; therefore, "good" teaching for some students might be disastrous for others. Examples could include such extremes as students who are gifted with students with mental retardation and their academic needs, or more subtle examples of students who benefit from explicit and structured instruction (i.e., students with learning disabilities) and those who benefit from open-ended, exploratory instruction.]

2.2

Essay. You are a special education teacher who is working with a general educator in a fourth grade class. Your team teacher tells you that your state is implementing a "standards test" at the end of this year; therefore, she wants to do less curriculum modification so that all students, including those with disabilities, will do well on the test. How do you respond?

[*Answer:* Answers should include acknowledgement of the importance of high standards for all students, yet the importance of the obligation to IEP requirements—specifically instructional objectives and delineated accommodations, the necessity of those modifications for the learning of your students, and the importance carefully examining each competency or skill area and making individual decision rather wholesale decisions on whether or not to modify.]

2.3

True/False. Effective early intervention programs have been shown by research to decrease the level of disability in some individuals.

[*Answer*: True.]

2.4

True/False. School-to-work activities begin at age 14 and continue post-high school.

[*Answer:* FALSE]

2.5

Essay. In "Early Warning, Timely Response: A Guide to Safe Schools," they identify some early warning signs. List three of these and then three preventative steps a school or teacher can do to reduce the likelihood of violence.

[*Answer:* Answers can include: social withdrawal, excessive feelings of isolation and being alone, excessive feelings of rejections, being a victim of violence, low school interest, feeling of being picked on or persecuted, patterns of impulsive hitting or bullying, uncontrolled anger, history of discipline problems, drug and alcohol abuse, association with a gang, inappropriate access to guns, etc. Preventative steps include: focus on academic achievement, involve families, emphasize positive relationships, create links with the community, discuss safety issues openly, demonstrate respect to all students, create ways for students to share their feelings, offer extended day services, etc.]

2.6

True/False. Students with disabilities are required by law to follow the same discipline rules as student without disabilities.

[*Answer*: False]

2.7

Multiple Choice. If the IEP team determines that a student's misbehavior is NOT related to his or her disability, then:
   a. Traditional discipline procedures established for students without disabilities are followed.
   b. A functional behavioral analysis must be conducted.
   c. The student is released from his or her IEP.
   d. The student may be disciplined using traditional discipline procedures, but is still ensured FAPE.

[*Answer:* D]

2.8

Essay. Write a several paragraph essay in which you summarize current trends and issues in special education. Be sure to include the following terms: normalization, full inclusion, continuum of alternative placements, disability rights movement, access to general education curriculum, and manifestation determination.

[*Answer:* Various responses.]

CHAPTER 3: MULTICULTURAL AND BILINGUAL ASPECTS OF SPECIAL EDUCATION

3.1

True/False. The identification of deviant behaviors can contribute to the reduction of undesired outcomes such as dropping out of school, incarceration, and being in abusive relationships.

[*Answer:* True]

3.2

True/False. The Urban Institute reports on issues relating to life in the inner cities.

[*Answer:* False]

3.3

True/False. Contextualization refers to the process of making abstractions concrete and relevant to students' lives.

[*Answer:* True]

3.4

Essay. In what ways to children's home experiences, particularly pre-school years, have on their performance in school. Be sure to identify key factors related to school success or failure. Then state 3 things schools can do to ameliorate some of these differences.

[*Answer:* Answers should include reference to research that has demonstrated that students, who lack exposure to language, literacy, and numeracy in the pre-school years, are at a deficit when they begin school. Solutions include: increased parent involvement through early intervention programs, provide effective instruction/experiences in the deficit areas, and having programs that reflect the culture of the students and families.]

3.5

Essay. List and provide examples of Bank's six components of culture.

[*Answer:* Bank's six components are: values and behavioral styles, language and dialects, nonverbal communication, awareness of one's cultural distinctiveness, frames of reference, and identification. Examples will vary.]

3.6

Essay. Teachers seeking to provide effective instruction for students with disabilities can face the "dilemma of difference" as described by Minow (1985). What instructional questions result from this situation?

[*Answer:* Answers should include the conflict the occurs in trying to treat all students the same and yet, recognizing and addressing differences.]

3.7

Essay. Describe four different things teachers should look for when evaluating linguistically and culturally appropriate materials.

[*Answer:* Answers should include: consideration of the students—language, style, and dialect; limitations—do strengths outweigh limitations?; possible adaptations; reflection of the community; cost, time, and expenses; etc.]

CHAPTER 4: MENTAL RETARDATION

4.1

Essay. Professionals have begun to recognize the limitations of using an IQ score as the sole criterion for the identification of mental retardation. What are some of the limitations of IQ and what additional information is sought when making these determinations?

[*Answer:* Limitations of IQ scores include: lack of consideration of adaptive skills, lack of stability if IQ scores over time and among tests, and lack of relationship between IQ scores and educational programming. Students should discuss the importance of collecting data on adaptive and functional skills.]

4.2

True/False. The Arc has developed position statements addressing various issues related to rights, treatment, services and programs for children and adults with mental retardation and their families to be used to influence public policy, guide media, and inform members of the community.

[*Answer:* True]

4.3

Essay. Describe the differences among "the era of institutionalization," "era of deinstitutionalization," and the "era of community." Include the following categories in your response: objectives, priorities, who is being served, service planning, and setting.

[*Answer:* Students should highlight the changes in how persons with mental retardation are viewed (from patient to client to citizen), where they received services (facility to continuum of options to selection of supports priority over placement decision), who controls the decisions (professional to team to individual), etc.]

4.4

Multiple choice. Genetic discrimination is defined as
    a. certain genes infected or damaged due to heredity.
    b. certain genes "at risk" and susceptible to environmental hazards.
    c. differential treatment of individuals based on actual or presumed genetic differences.
    d. differential treatment of individuals who are more likely to be responsive to gene therapy.

[*Answer:* C]

4.5

Essay. Pretend you are a parent of a child with mental retardation. Write a statement on what you goals—educational and social you have for your child. Include factors relating to intellectual, skill, and social growth opportunities.

[*Answer:* Responses will vary.]

4.6

True/False. IQ scores are socially constructed and therefore, are not longer used in the identification of mental retardation.

[*Answer:* False]

4.7

True/False. Research has shown that IQ scores can be influenced through early intervention and appropriate education.

[*Answer:* True]

4.8

True/False. Since adaptive behaviors are largely developmental, it is possible to describe a person's adaptive behavior as an age-equivalent score.

[*Answer:* True]

4.9

Multiple Choice. Functional academics refers to
    a. academics that can be directly linked independent functioning

    b.   academics that lead to a job as a laborer
    c.   academics that support students as they move to postsecondary schooling
    d.   the development of skills that involve gross motor skills

[*Answer:* A]

4.10

Short Answer. Write three domain goal areas that a person with MR might have. Under each domain, write two specific goals.

[Answer: Possible domain categories include: academic, domestic, leisure, self-help, community living, and vocational skills. Specific goals will vary but should be operationalized and measurable.]

4.11

True/False. Supported employment is a workplace where adults who are disabled earn at least minimum wage and receive ongoing assistance from a specialist or job coach.

[*Answer:* True]

CHAPTER 5: LEARNING DISABILITIES

5.1

Short Answer. List four components of Direct Instruction.

[*Answer:* Answers can include: based on task analysis, systematic, fast-paced, drill and practice, scripted, hand signals for prompts, choral responding, and immediate corrective feedback.]

5.2

Short Answer. Dr. Hallahan, in his article "We Need More Intensive Instruction," discusses some of the challenges to effective collaboration. List 3 challenges to collaboration.

[*Answer:* Challenges include majority of time spent on consulting rather than teaching, effectiveness of instruction diminished due to large numbers of students, difficulties in establishing a mutually supportive relationship, outcome measures for students with LD can be disappointing.]

5.3

Essay. Discuss the legal conflict that can occur between the provision of an appropriate education and LRE as stated by LDA.

[*Answer:* LDA believes that decisions regarding educational placement of students with learning disabilities must be based first on the needs of each individual student and second on the legislative requirement for LRE.]

5.4

True/False. Students with learning disabilities tend to lack appropriate coping strategies for dealing with stress.

[*Answer:* True]

5.5
Multiple Choice. Which of the following assessments is NOT and example of authentic assessment:
    a. Essay
    b. Portfolio
    c. Experiments and their results
    d. Informal Reading Inventory

[*Answer:* D]

5.6
True/False. Direct Instruction, shown by extensive research to bring about long-term academic gains, is among the most popular way to teach students with learning disabilities to read.

[*Answer:* False]

5.7
Essay. Define self-determination and discuss how it relates to students with learning disabilities.

[*Answer:* Self-determination involves knowing what one wants and understanding what is necessary to bring it about. Students with disabilities typically lack these skills and must be explicitly taught them. Self-determination becomes more important as students get older and need to advocate for themselves more frequently. Self-determination has recently be recognized as one the overriding goals of transition programming.]

5.8
Activity. Write a transition plan for Steve.

[*Answer:* Plans should include: statement of parent and student involvement, goal setting, delineation of goal and objectives, list of activities to support goals, method of assessment of progress toward goals, list of agencies and services necessary, and transition counseling (if deemed appropriate).]

CHAPTER 6: ATTENTION DEFICIT HYPERACTIVITY DISORDER

6.1
Multiple Choice. Which of the following treatment options is NOT advocated for students with ADHD:
    a. Feingold diet
    b. Structured environment
    c. Psychostimulants
    d. Direct instruction
    e.
[*Answer:* A]

6.2
Fact/Myth. A poor diet, such as high levels of sugar and/or food additives, can cause ADD.

[*Answer:* Myth]

6.3

True/False. According to the 1997 Amendments to IDEA, AD/HD is now its own disability category.

[*Answer:* False—students with ADHD still are eligible under the OHI category, but ADHD is now specifically list under OHI]

6.4

Short Answer. Describe three reasons for the recent increase in the number of students identified at OHI.

[*Answer:* Answers should include: increased awareness of AD/HD and therefore, classification under the OHI category, potential over identification of boys, more accurate reporting, social/cultural changes that have put more students at risk]

6.5

Short Answer. In what ways can teachers present information that is sensitive to the various perspectives of the participants in the multi-disciplinary team?

[*Answer:* Responses will vary. Appropriate answers could include soliciting information for all participants in a neutral mode prior to the meeting, using non-emotive language, preparing parents for the meeting with a pre-meeting conference, etc.]

6.6

True/False. Once a qualified physician has made the diagnosis of ADHD, the child automatically qualifies for special education serves.

[*Answer:* False—the decision is still made by the team and includes other assessment documentation such as child's history, checklists completed by teachers, parents, etc., and classroom observation documentation]

6.7

Multiple Choice. The frontal lobes are responsible for:
   a. Broca's Area
   b. Executive functions
   c. Language
   d. Hyperactivity

[*Answer:* B]

6.8

Essay. Describe a contingency-based self-management program.

[*Answer:* Answers will vary. Key features include: students keep track of their own behaviors and rewards/consequences are delivered based upon performance]

6.9

Multiple Choice. An "coach" for someone with ADHD is someone who:
   a. provides emotional support and practical advice
   b. track medication dosages and behavioral responses
   c. provides a self-management program for the client
   d. works on decreasing ADHD symptoms through diet and exercise

[Answer: A]

CHAPTER 7: EMOTIONAL OR BEHAVIORAL DISORDERS

7.1

<u>True/False.</u> A conduct disorder is a persistent pattern of behavior that involves violation of the rights of others.

[Answer: True]

7.2

<u>True/False.</u> In the Federal definition of emotional disturbed, educational performance is clearly defined.

[Answer: False]

7.3

<u>Short Answer.</u> What are the five factors identified by researchers relating to youth violence and delinquency.

[Answer: (1) the mother and/or the father has been arrested, (2) the child has been a client of child protection, (3) one or more family transitions have occurred (death, divorce, trauma, family upheaval), (4) the youth has received special education services, and (5) the child has a history of early and/or severe antisocial behavior.]

7.4

<u>True/False.</u> Pharmacological interventions (medication) can improve the behavioral and cognitive functioning of individuals with autism.

[Answer: True]

7.5

<u>Short answer.</u> Define the following terms, as they were presented in the NAMI article on seclusion and restraint: control of the environment, coercion, and punishment.

[Answer: **control of the environment** = actions taken by facilities to curtail individual behavior to avoid having to use adequate staffing or clinical interventions; **coercion** = designed solely to force the patient to comply with the staff's wishes; or **punishment** = actions taken by staff to punish or penalize patients.]

7.6

<u>Short Answer.</u> List 3 early warning signs associated with suicide.

[Answer: Responses can include any of the following: recent loss, change in personality, change in behaviors, change in sleep patterns, change in eating habits, fear of losing control, diminished sexual interest, and low self-esteem.]

7.7

<u>Essay.</u> List and discuss 3 ways that Kauffman believes schools and society at large engage in the "prevention of prevention."

[*Answer:* Possible answers include: an overriding concern for labels, objecting to a medical model of services, preferring false negatives to false positives, calling special education ineffective, misconstruing the least restrictive and least intrusive intervention, complaining of the costs associated with special education, maintaining developmental optimism, denouncing disproportionate identification, defending diversity, and denying or dodging deviance.]

CHAPTER 8: COMMUNICATION DISORDERS

8.1
True/False. All communication disorders involve speech.

[*Answer:* False]

8.2
Multiple Choice. Appropriate speech goals include all of the following EXCEPT:
- a. articulation
- b. fluency
- c. pragmatics
- d. producing voice

[*Answer:* C—pragmatics would be a language goal]

8.3
Short Answer. Respond to the following question posed by ASHA: How will the need to "address general education/curriculum " affect the role of the SLP?

[*Answer:* "Framing benchmarks in curriculum language will ensure that both the special educator and the classroom teacher are addressing the objective, and that the effect of the child's disability on achievement is the focus of special education services." (from the ASHA web site)]

8.4
Essay. Describe 3 ways in which teachers can promote language development in their classes.

[*Answer:* Responses can include: instruction in grammar, verb tense production, lengthening sentences, asking questions, and vocabulary development.]

8.5
Essay. Define efficiency and authenticity in terms of augmentative and alternative means of communication. Then discuss why "authenticity" can carry ethical ramifications as well.

[*Answer:* Efficiency refers to the speed and the easy with which one can communicate; Authenticity refers to the fact that the message/communication comes from the person with the disability. Authenticity is important because it would be a violation of a persons rights to, in essence, "put words in their mouth."]

8.6
Essay. In what ways can models of service delivery that include the prescription of expensive technology, and frequent visits to several different members of a healthcare services delivery team, e.g., speech-language

pathologists, physical and occupational therapists, rehabilitation engineers, computer access specialists, and so forth be counter to the culture of the family.

[*Answer:* Responses will vary, but could address issues of cultural mistrust, financial resources, views of health, disability, and/or technology, and family/community values.]

8.7
True/False. The sounds produced by digital hearing aids sound remarkably similar to the hearing of people without hearing loss.

[*Answer:* False]

CHAPTER 9: HEARING IMPAIRMENT

9.1
True/False. Deaf culture refers to the believe that deafness is not a "pathology" rather it way of living, communicating, and interacting with the world.

[*Answer:* True]

9.2
Short Answer. Name 2 ways ADA can protect the rights of someone who is deaf or hard of hearing.

[*Answer:* Appropriate answers can include: availability of an interpreter, access to TDD or captioning technology, protection against discriminatory practices, protection from exclusion in schools or from a job due to deafness, access to medical treatment—hospitals must have communication options for the deaf]

9.3
True/False. The deaf population in the United States is approximately .5%.

[*Answer:* True]

9.4
Essay. Describe cochlear implants and summarize the key points in the debates that surround them.

[*Answer:* Responses should include surgical procedure for implant, overview of how the implants work, and then discussion related to whether or not deafness is a disability or a characteristic and questions related to effectiveness of the implant.]

9.5
True/False. Some people within the deaf community believe that too much mainstreaming is a threat to the Deaf culture.

[*Answer:* True]

9.6

Essay. Describe how the experiences of a Gallaudet student would be similar to yours? How would it be different? In what ways does Gallaudet prepare students for post-university life that is similar to your institution? Different?

[*Answer:* Responses will vary]

CHAPTER 10: VISUAL IMPAIRMENT

10.1

True/False. Braille is of no value for those with low vision.

[*Answer:* False]

10.2

Short Answer. Describe the "Digital Talking Book" and how it can transform the reading experience for people who are blind or with low vision.

[*Answer:* Digital Talking Books can provide full text that can be automatically displayed in Braille or in large print fonts. Books are also "read" by narrative and can be listened to.]

10.3

Short Answer. Define "itinerant teacher" and explain why this term is usually associated with the provision of services for students with visual impairments.

[*Answer:* An itinerant teacher is a special educator who works with students (and their teachers) in several different schools. Due to the low numbers of students with visual impairments, itinerant teachers are usually the most cost effective way to provide services to a number of students across a district or region.]

10.4

Short Answer. What is diabetic retinopathy and in what ways does it affect vision.

[*Answer:* Diabetic retinopathy is a condition resulting from lack of blood supplied to the retina. (It is also the fastest-growing cause of blindness). Vision would look like someone had blacked out parts of a scene.]

10.5

Essay. In the "Questions From Kids About Blindness" article, many questions are posed and answered. Describe two things you learned about from reading this article.

[*Answer:* Answers will vary but can include: How do blind people…identify food, clothes, money; play card games; use a cane; cook; tell time; go to school; and cross the street.]

10.6

Essay. How does the law help people with visual disabilities get access to alternative print materials?

[*Answer:* Students are protected under IDEA, which means at no cost to the individual (or family) accessible materials should be provided. ADA allows for reasonable accommodations in the workplace, which may include note takers, readers, Braille, audio recordings, and large-print materials.]

10.7
True/False. Most people who are blind would rather have access to jobs and independent living than medical treatment and counseling.

[*Answer:* True]

CHAPTER 11: PHYSICAL DISABILITIES

11.1
Essay. In the debate between individual rights and protection of individuals, where do you stand and why?

[*Answer:* Response will vary according to individual beliefs.]

11.2
True/False. The highest rate of TBI is among males, ages 25-35.

[*Answer:* False—male, youths]

11.3
True/False. "Congenital" cerebral palsy means that the condition is related to the development and childbearing processes.

[*Answer:* True]

11.4
True/False. The relationship between Spina Bifida and latex allergies is clearly understood.

[*Answer:* False]

11.5
Short Answer. Describe the characteristics of children with Fetal Alcohol Syndrome and some educational considerations.

[*Answer:* Fetal Alcohol Syndrome is an umbrella term that encompasses mental and physical birth defects that can include mental retardation, growth deficiencies, central nervous system dysfunction, craniofacial abnormalities and behavioral maladjustment's. Educational interventions can include: instruction in organizational strategies, use of task analysis when planning for instruction, creating a structured and consistent learning environment, and providing opportunities to strengthen self-determination.]

11.6
Essay. Describe the relationship between teenage pregnancies and children with disabilities. What are some ways to prevent teen mothers giving birth to kids with disabilities.

[*Answer:* Teen mothers are at a greater risk of giving birth to premature or low-birth weight babies due to inadequate prenatal care, having infections during pregnancy, poor nutrition, and anemia. Prevention can include access to better health care, better nutrition, and avoidance of pregnancy.]

11.7
True/False. People with disabilities are excluded from mainstream sporting competitions, such as the Olympics or professional golf, but can participate in a variety of alternative competitions.

[*Answer:* False]

CHAPTER 12: SPECIAL GIFTS AND TALENTS

12.1
True/False. A person with special gifts does everything well.

[*Answer:* False]

12.2
Short Answer. What are the difficulties with the identification of learning disabilities or ADHD comorbidity with giftedness?

[*Answer:* Student who are gifted and also have learning disabilities or ADHD, are often not identified as accurately or as early in their lives as their non-gifted peers. Early diagnosis and intervention are important for helping these students get access to services that would help reduce some of their learning difficulties.]

12.3
True/False. Unlike students with disabilities, gifted students do not have a continuum of placement options— once identified gifted students receive services through separate classes.

[*Answer:* False]

12.4
Short Answer. Name three different intelligence tests.

[*Answer:* Answers can include Slosson Intelligence Test, Kaufman Adolescent and Adult Intelligence Test, Social Intelligence Test: George Washington University Series, Culture Fair Intelligence Test, or Non-Verbal Intelligence Tests for Deaf and Hearing Subjects]

12.5
Essay. Do you believe that the issues related to grouping practices (i.e., heterogeneous vs. homogenous ability grouping) differ for students with disabilities than the issues for students with hyperabilities? Why or why not?
[Answer: Answers will vary depending on student perspective]

12.6
Short Answer. What is the difference between acceleration and enrichment?

[*Answer:* Acceleration involves moving a child into a grade or placement ahead of his or her age peers. Enrichment means that students are engaged in projects or activities that specifically designed to challenge and stimulate talented students.]

12.7
Essay. If you were to design an accelerated program, what kinds of characteristics would you look for in potential candidates?

[*Answer:* In order for students to be successful in accelerated programs they must possess emotional stability and maturity (as they will be with students who are older—sometime 4 years), they must have a strong work ethic (even though a student may be very bright, if they do not apply themselves, the program will not be successful), and they should posses specific talents in the area of specialization or interest.]

CHAPTER 13: PARENTS AND FAMILIES

13.1
Essay. In what ways can teachers plan for the involvement of parents. Include specific examples.

[*Answer:* Responses will vary according to student's perspective.]

13.2
Essay. Why were terms like defective, idiot, and imbecile replaced with the word disability or more generally with "people first" language.

[*Answer:* Historical terms of defect, idiot, and imbecile are more value laden than current terms. Additionally, the terms "dehumanized" the individual—often he or she was replaced with the pronoun "it"—and therefore, excusing people from any moral obligation to the rights of that person.]

13.3
Short Answer. What things should one take into consideration when responding to an uniformed, layperson who has made an inappropriate statement about a person with a disability or disabilities in general?

[*Answer:* Answers can include: the relationship you have with this person, the background of the person, how responsive you believe they might be to "correct" information, how much time you want to spend educating this person, etc.]

13.4
Short Answer. Define "family systems theory."

[*Answer:* Family systems theory states that events that affect one member of the family also affect the other members, thus there is a reciprocal relationship among family members. Treatment and education should involve all members of the family.]

13.5
True/False. Professionals are always in the best position to help families of people with disabilities.

[*Answer:* False]

SPED 1010: Introduction to Exceptionality
Fall 2000, Peabody College
Vanderbilt University

Kristin A. Lundgren, Ph.D.
Box 328 Peabody College
Office: 302A MRL
(615) 322-8179

kristin.lundgren@vanderbilt.edu
Office hours: T R 9-10; W 10-11
Room: Mayborn 204
Days and times: MWF 9:10-10:00

Course Description

Examines issues and trends in special education and overviews the characteristics of persons with disabilities. Explores essential issues and theories relating to special education and the development of exceptional persons with special attention to normal and atypical human development. Addresses multi-cultural, humanistic, and legal issues.

Course Objectives (from the Council for Exceptional Children)

I. Philosophical, Historical, and Legal Foundations of Special Education
- Identify models, theories, and philosophies that provide the basis for special education including an historical perspective. (CC1, K1)
- Discuss variations in beliefs, traditions, and values across and within cultures and their effects on relationships among the child, family, and school. (CC1, K2)
- Become familiar with issues in definitions and identifying individuals with exceptional learning needs, including those from culturally and linguistically diverse populations. (CC1, K3)
- Discuss legal rights related to assessment, eligibility, and placement within a continuum of services. (CC1, K4)
- Identify the rights and responsibilities of parents, students, teachers and other professionals, and schools as they relate to individual learning needs. (CC1, K5)

II. Characteristics of Learners
- Identify similarities and differences among individuals with and without disabilities including cognitive, physical, cultural, social, and emotional needs. (CC2, K1)
- Identify similarities and differences among individual with disabilities including levels of severity and multiple disabilities. (CC2, K2)
- Discuss the characteristics of normal, delayed, and disordered communication patterns of individuals with exceptional learning needs. (CC2, K3)
- Explain the effects a disability may have on an individual's life. (CC2, K4)
- Discuss the characteristics and effects of the cultural and environmental milieu of the child and the family including cultural and linguistic diversity, socioeconomic level, abuse/neglect, and substance abuse. (CC2, K5)
- Describe the effects of various medications on the educational, cognitive, physical, social, and emotional behavior of individuals with exceptionalities. (CC2, K6)
- Discuss the educational implications of various disabilities. (CC2, K7)
- Access information on various cognitive, communication, physical, cultural, social, and emotional conditions of individuals with exceptional learning needs. (CC2, S1)

Course Objectives (continued)

III. Assessment, Diagnosis, and Evaluation
- Explain the screening, prereferral, referral, and classification procedures used in identifying individuals with exceptional learning needs. (CC3, K4)

IV. Instructional Content and Practice
- Discuss cultural perspectives influencing the relationship among families, schools, and communities as related to effective instruction for individuals with exceptional learning needs. (CC4, K7)

V. Managing Student Behavior and Social Interactions
- Discuss laws, policies, and ethical principles regarding behavior management planning and implementation. (CC6, K1)
- Discuss teacher attitudes and behaviors that influence behavior of individuals with exceptional learning needs. (CC6, K3)
- Discuss strategies for preparing individuals to live harmoniously and productively in a multiclass, multiethnic, multicultural, and multinational world. (CC6, K6)

VI. Communication and Collaborative Partnerships
- Discuss culturally responsive factors that promote effective communication and collaboration with individuals, families, school personnel, and community members. (CC7, K1)
- Identify concerns of families of individuals with exceptional learning needs and strategies to help address these concerns. (CC7, K2)
- Discuss ethical practices for confidential communication to others about individuals with exceptional learning needs. (CC7, K5)

VII. Professionalism and Ethical Practices
- Describe personal cultural biases and differences that affect one's teaching. (CC8, K1)
- Explain the importance of the teacher serving as a model for individuals with exceptional learning needs. (CC8, K2)

Text

     Hallahan, D. P., & Kauffman, J. M. (2000). Exceptional learners: Introduction to special education, 8th edition. Boston, MA: Allyn & Bacon.

Required Readings (on reserve at the library)

     Fuchs, D., & Fuchs, L. (1995). What's "special" about special education? Phi Delta Kappan, 76, 522-30.

     Gersten, R. (1998). Recent advances in instructional research for students with learning disabilities: An overview. Learning Disabilities Practice, 13, 162-170.

     Kauffman, J. M. (1999). How we prevent the prevention of emotional and behavioral disorders. Exceptional Children, 65(4), 448-468.

Newcomer, J. & Zirkel, P. A. (1999). An analysis of judicial outcomes of special education cases. Exceptional Children, 65(4), 469-480.

MacMillan, D. L., & Reschly, D. J. (1998). Overrepresentation of minority students: the case for greater specificity or reconsideration of the variables examined. Journal of Special Education, 32, 15-24.

Reschly, D. (1996). Identification and assessment of children with disabilities. The Future of Children: Special Education for Children with Disabilities, 6(1), 40-53.

Walker, H. (1998). Youth violence: Society's problem. Available: http://www.oslc.org/InTheNews/society.html (August, 2000).

Worrall, R. S. (1990). Detecting health fraud in the field of learning disabilities. Journal of Learning Disabilities, 23, 207-212.

Requirements

Assignment	Points	Date Due
Attendance and in-class activities	50 pts.	**on-going**
Volunteer Work	50 pts.	**10/16 (mid-term log and journal check)** **12/4 (final log and journal due)**
Movie Review	50 pts.	**9/25**
Mid-Term Exam	75 pts.	**10/11**
Web Page	50 pts.	**11/13**
Final Exam	75 pts.	**12/18 9:00 a.m.**

Grading System

Grades in this class will be based on the number of points that the student obtains during the semester:

A: 326- 350 total points
B: 291 - 325 total points
C: 256 - 290 total points
D: 221 - 255 total points
F: Less than 221 total points

Vanderbilt's Honor Code governs all work in this course.

Assignments

<u>Attendance</u>

Attendance at all class sessions is required. Participation in class discussions and activities is an integral part of this course. Your reflections on the assigned readings and ability to create personal relevance will add to the overall objectives of the course.

Throughout the semester, students will participate in in-class activities. Attendance will be taken during 10 of these activities and students will be awarded 5 attendance points for each activity (for a total of 50 attendance points).

<u>Volunteer Work</u>

Each student is required to volunteer for a local agency serving persons with disabilities. Agencies are excited about having you volunteer and there are numerous organizations and available times for you to volunteer. Students will work with the TA to arrange a site and schedule for their 15 hours. Although the TA will assist with initial arrangements and provide support throughout the semester, students are responsible for making sure they meet the minimum time requirements. The contact number for placement information is **322-8175**.

Students must complete a minimum of 15 hours of volunteer work by the end of the semester and keep a journal of each day's experiences. Grades for the volunteer work will be based upon the completion of hours and the journal requirements. Journals should include the following information:

1. General
    a. Log of dates and times you were at the site (see attached)
    b. Description of the site and services provided
    c. Description of the population served
2. For each visit
    a. What did you do?
    b. With whom did you work? Insights and observations about the people and interactions.
    c. General observations about changes in your perceptions, information you would like to have, information you learned, and/or connections to class work.
    d. Any suggestions or comments to the instructor or TA.

A minimum of 10 entries is required (see Volunteer Work Rubric for details). This assignment is worth 50 points.

<u>Assignment I: Movie Review</u>

The purpose of this activity is to help acquaint you with ways in which individuals with disabilities are depicted in films. View the film with an air of "healthy skepticism," paying particular attention to any connections that can be made with materials we have been studying and issues we have discussed in class. Write a 4 page (6 page limit) critical analysis of the film in which you highlight the film's strengths and weaknesses in terms of accuracy of information, realistic portrayal of people with disabilities, timeliness of the message, and overall tone of the film.

The following films are approved (if you select a film that is not on the pre-approved list, check with the instructor before completing the assignment):

Children of a Lesser God	Rain Man	Dominick and Eugene
The Heart is a Lonely Hunter	Miracle Worker	Charly
What's Eating Gilbert Grape	Nell	Mask
One Flew Over the Cuckoo's Nest	My Left Foot	Shine
A Day of the Death of Joe Egg	Of Mice and Men	Sling Blade
A Brief History of Time	Ordinary People	The Elephant Man
Born of the Fourth of July	The Waterdance	

This assignment is worth 50 points.

Assignment II: Informational Web Site

Students will design a web page that provides information about a specific disability category. Students may work independently or with a partner for this assignment. The purpose of this task is for students to conduct an in-depth exploration of a particular disability and then synthesis and summarize the information to share with others. Students must consult 7 references in addition to the text (of those 7 required references, only 2 may be web sites*). Appropriate resources include:

- **Journals** (such as, Exceptional Children, Teaching Exceptional Children, Journal of Special Education, Education and Training in Mental Retardation, Journal of Learning Disabilities, Behavioral Disorders, Education and Treatment of Children, Journal of the Association for Persons with Severe Handicaps, Intervention in School and Clinic)
- **Books** (textbooks, trade books on specific topics, etc.)
- **Web sites** (advocacy organizations, topical sites, parent groups, school sites, university sites, federal/state/local special education organizations, research sites, etc.)

It is assumed that students will consult more than 2 web sites (and probably link to several as well), but only 2 of those can count toward the 7 required outside references.

All web pages should include the following sections:

Section	Type of Information
Home Page	○ Title of your presentation and name of author(s) ○ Abstract (this should include a summary of your content, potential audiences, and statements related to conclusions you reached after constructing the site) ○ Table of Contents/Site Map (each section title should be linked to the appropriate page)
Characteristics	○ Description of characteristics ○ Information related to identification
Treatment Considerations	○ Medical considerations ○ Early intervention

Section	Type of Information
Educational Implications	o Research on educational methods that are effective for the population o Descriptions of program(s) o Suggestions for teachers
Parents and Families	o Legal Rights o Concerns specifically for families
Resources	o Books o Videos o Organizations
References*	o Complete list of references (use APA style)

*Each section should include the appropriate references within text in the appropriate section and then on the Reference section. For guidelines and examples of how to reference using APA, go to Purdue University's Online Writing Lab:
http://owl.english.purdue.edu/handouts/research/r_apa.html

   Notes on page construction: Text found on other web sites may not be "borrowed" directly (that is, you can't cut and paste stuff found on other pages—that is plagiarism). You may link to other sites or paraphrase the information and then provide appropriate references. The same is true for pictures—borrowing them violates copyright laws. Links to free pictures and icons (gifs) can be found on our class web site, along with other information regarding "netiquette."

Mid-Term and Final Exams
   There will be two exams (of the multiple choice, T/F, short answer, and essay question variety). The mid-term exam will include material from the text, readings, and class presentations of chapters covered up to that point. The focus (~70%) of the final exam will be on material covered during the last half of the year, but there will be some questions that address information from the first half. Each exam is worth 75 points.

Tentative Class Schedule

Date	Topic	Reading	Media & Activities	Assignment Due	Competency
8/30	Introduction/Syllabus				
9/1	Disability vs. Handicap	Chapter 1			CC2, K4; CC8, K2
9/4	History		*Weblink 1.9: "Inventing a Poster Child" (NPR series)*		CC1, K1;
9/6	Current Trends and Issues	Chapter 2	Weblink 2.2: Renaissance & LD OnLine "Educating Peter" (video)		CC1, K3; CC4, K7; CC1; K4
9/8	IDEA, ADA, and Section 504 of the Rehabilitation Act		http://www.apa.org/psychnet/disabilities.html (10th anniversary of ADA)		CC1, K4; CC1, K5; CC2, K7
9/11	Legislation	Newcomer & Zirkel (1999)	*Weblink 1.7: Compare IDEA, ADA, and 504*		CC1, K4; CC6, K1;
9/13	Identification	Reschly (1996)			CC1, K3; CC2, K5; CC3, K4
9/15	Mental Retardation	Chapter 4	*Weblink 4.1 ARC position statements*		CC2, K1; CC2, K4; CC1, K5
9/18	Mental Retardation		"Best Boy" (video)		CC2, K7
9/20	Learning Disabilities	Chapter 5			CC2, K1; CC2, K4;
9/22	Learning Disabilities		"F.A.T. City" (video)		CC1, K1; CC2, K4; CC2, S1
9/25	Instructional Considerations of LDs	Gersten (1998)	*Weblink 5.1 LD OnLine: "We need more intensive instruction"*	**Movie Review Due**	CC2, K7

Date	Topic	Reading	Media	Assignment	Standards
9/27	Guest Lecture: Lynn Fuchs (PALS and CBM)	Fuchs & Fuchs (1995)			CC2, K7
9/29	Attention Deficit Disorder	Chapter 6	"ADD/ADHD/LD" (LD/LA video) *Weblink 6.1 CHADD*		CC2, K4; CC2, K6; CC2, K7
10/2	Emotional or Behavioral Disorders	Chapter 7			CC2, K1; CC2, K4; CC2, K6
10/4	School Violence	Hill Walker's article "Youth Violence: Society's Problem"	*Weblink 7.8 Youth Violence: Society's Problem*		CC2, S1; CC6, K3
10/6	Preventing Prevention and Educational Considerations for EBD	Kauffman (1999)	*Audio 7.2 Preventing Prevention*		CC1, K2; CC2, K7; CC6, K1; CC6, K3;
10/9	Review for Exam				
10/11	**Mid-term Exam**			**EXAM**	
10/13	Guest Lecture: Dan Reschly (overrepresentation)	MacMillan & Reschly (1998)			CC6, K3; CC1, K3
10/16	Multicultural Issues	Chapter 3	*Weblink 3.2 CREDE*	**Mid-term Log and Journal Check**	CC1, K2; CC2, K7; CC4, K7; CC6, K6
10/18	Communication Disorders	Chapter 8	*Audio 8.2 Problems for All of Us*		CC2, K1; CC2, K3; CC2, K4
10/20	Speech and Language Issues				CC2, K7;

Date	Topic	Reading	Media / Weblink	Assignment	Standards
10/23	Assistive Technology		*Weblink 11.21 Assistive Devices*		CC2, K3
10/25	Guest Lecturer: Wendy Sapp (visual impairments)		*Weblink 10.12 How Do You?*		CC2, K7
10/27	Visual Impairments	Chapter 10			CC2, K1; CC2, K4;
10/30	Autism				CC2, K2; CC2, K3
11/1	Facilitative Communication	Worrall (1990)	Frontline Film "Prisoners of Silence"		CC8, K2
11/3	Hearing Impairments	Chapter 9			CC2, K1; CC2, K4;
11/6	Guest Lecture: Gail Zika (Hearing Impairments)		"For a Deaf Son" (video)		CC2, K7
11/8	Gifted and Talented	Chapter 12			CC2, K1; CC2, K4
11/10	Gifted and Talented		*Audio 12.2 Acceleration–When To Use It?*		CC2, K7;
11/13	Share Web Pages			**Web Pages Due**	CC2, S1
11/15	Share Web Pages				
11/17	Parents and Families	Chapter 13	*Weblink 13.1 Disability Archives (NPR program)*		CC2, K5; CC4, K7; CC7, K2
			Thanksgiving Holiday 11/20–11/24		
11/27	Understanding perspectives		*Video 6.2 Eric*		CC7, K1; CC1, K1
11/29	IEPs				CC3, K4; CC7, K5

Date	Topic	Reading	Activity/Weblink	Due	Standards
12/1	IEP—Activity (What's Best for Matthew)		What's Best for Mathew (CD Rom)		CC3, K4; CC7, K5
12/4	Physical Disabilities/Motor Impairments	Chapter 11		**Final Journal and Log Due**	CC2, K2; CC2, K4
12/6	Other Conditions that Affect Health or Physical Ability		*Weblink 11.13 National Organization on Fetal Alcohol Syndrome*		CC2, K2; CC2, K6
12/8	Pulling It All Together				
12/11	Review for the final				
			Exams 12/18 9:00–11:00 a.m.		

Volunteer Log

Name: _____

Volunteer site: _____

Date	Time in/Time out	Total Number of Volunteer Hours	Initial from Supervisor

Mid-term approval from TA: _____

Final approval from TA: _____

Volunteer Work Rubric

Grade	Time Requirements	Journal Requirements	Overall Quality
A (45-50 pts)	15 (or more) hours	10 (or more) entries	• Log with mid-term and final signatures • General section clearly described and accurate • Reflections that demonstrate consideration of personal assumptions, biases, and insights (that is, growth is evident) • Connections to class discussions—highlighting issues and themes (In what ways is this a part of early intervention or lead to effective transition OR is contrary to what we have talked about as best practices?) *We laughed; we cried; it moved us.*
B (40-44 pts)	15 hours	10 entries	• Log with mid-term and final signatures • General section includes all necessary details • Reflective statements that demonstrate consideration of issues discussed in class *Three stars: Good plot but not much character development.*
C (35-39 pts)	10-14 hours	8-9 entries	• Log with final signature and mid-term plan (statement of how hours will be met) • General section included but not well defined • Statements on visits more a summary of events than reflective statements *Been there; done that.*
D (34 pts or fewer)	Less than 10 hours	Less than 8 entries	• Log partially complete • Brief statements regarding visits • Obviously completed in a hurry (say, the night before it was due) *Where's the beef?*